NEVER SPREAD LIKE MARMALADE
Stories of Wit and Humour

Never Spread like Marmalade

Stories of Wit and Humour

Compiled by

MARGARET HAINSON

THE BODLEY HEAD

LONDON SYDNEY

TORONTO

This collection © Margaret Hainson 1975
ISBN 0 370 10946 5
Printed and bound in Great Britain for
The Bodley Head Ltd
9 Bow Street, London WC2E 7AL
by Redwood Burn Ltd, Trowbridge
Set in Monotype Baskerville
by Gloucester Typesetting Co Ltd
First published 1975

For K,
whether she likes it or not

COMPILER'S NOTE

For those who are concerned about such things, the title of this book is taken from a quotation by Noël Coward. 'Wit', the Master is reported to have said, 'ought to be a glorious treat, like caviar. It should be served in small elegant portions; never spread it about like marmalade.'

So it is not the purpose of this anthology that it should be read at one sitting, or even two or three, but rather that it should be dipped into at random or read a story or two at a time. The reader is therefore warned about exceeding the dose stated.

MARGARET HAINSON

CONTENTS

ACKNOWLEDGMENTS

'The Great Detergent Premium Race' from *Just Add Water and Stir* by Pierre Berton. Reprinted by permission of the Canadian Publishers, McClelland and Stewart Ltd, Toronto.

'To the Rankling La' from *The Ascent of Rum Doodle* by W. E. Bowman, published by Max Parrish, London.

'The Night the Bed Fell' by James Thurber. Published in London in *Vintage Thurber*, copyright © Hamish Hamilton 1963. Published in New York by Harper and Row in *My Life and Hard Times*. Copyright © 1933, 1961 James Thurber. Originally printed in *The New Yorker*.

'Car Episode' being Chapter 2, 'Jack', of *Hang on a Minute Mate* by Barry Crump. Reprinted by permission of A. H. & A. W. Reed Ltd, Wellington.

'The Arrival of Blackman's Warbler' from *Those Were the Days* by A. A. Milne. Reprinted by permission of Curtis Brown Ltd, London, acting on behalf of C. R. Milne.

'The Standard of Living' from *The Collected Dorothy Parker* (Duckworth, London) and *The Portable Dorothy Parker* (Viking Press, New York). Copyright 1941 by Dorothy Parker. Copyright © renewed 1969 by Lillian Hellman. Originally appeared in *The New Yorker*. Reprinted by permission of the publishers.

' "Q." A Psychic Pstory of the Psupernatural' from *Nonsense Novels* by Stephen Leacock. Reprinted by permission of the Bodley Head Ltd, London, and the Canadian Publishers, McClelland and Stewart Ltd, Toronto.

'Motion Study Tonsils' from *Cheaper by the Dozen* by Frank B. Gilbreth, Jr, and Ernestine Gilbreth Carey. Copyright © 1963. Reprinted by permission of William Heinemann Ltd, London, and Thomas Y. Crowell Company, Inc., New York.

'Tooking for a Lowel' from *Patrick Campbell's Omnibus*. Copyright Patrick Campbell.

'The Sportsmen of Scowle' by Bernard Hollowood. Reprinted by permission of *Punch*.

'The Strange Case of Mr Donnybrook's Boredom' from *Bed Riddance* by Ogden Nash. Reprinted by permission of Andre Deutsch Ltd, London, and Little, Brown & Co., Boston. Copyright © 1936 by Ogden Nash. Copyright © renewed 1964 by Ogden Nash.

'First Confession' by Frank O'Connor. Reprinted by permission of A. D. Peters and Co.

'Safe and Soundproof' by Joan Aiken. Copyright © Joan Aiken 1959.

'The Advantages of Cheese as a Travelling Companion' from *Three Men in a Boat* by Jerome K. Jerome. Reprinted by permission of J. M. Dent and Sons Ltd, London.

'The Scholarly Mouse' from *The Scholarly Mouse and Other Tales* by Dal Stivens. Reprinted by permission of Dal Stivens.

'Tobias the Terrible' from *Runyon on Broadway* by Damon Runyon. Reprinted by permission of Constable and Co. Ltd, London, and American Play Company, New York.

'The lamps are going out all over Europe' from *You Can't Have Your Kayak and Heat It* by Frank Muir and Denis Norden. Reprinted by permission of Eyre Methuen Ltd, London.

'The Story of Wong Ts'in and the Willow Plate Embellishment' from *Kai Lung's Golden Hours* by Ernest Bramah. Reprinted by permission of Geoffrey Bles, London.

'A Strategy Suit with a Jelly Pocket' from *Cock-a-doodle-don't* by Ivor Cutler. Reprinted by permission of Dennis Dobson, London.

The Great Detergent Premium Race

by Pierre Berton

The idea was born originally in the mind of J. Algernon
Krief, a junior account executive with the advertising
agency of Carstairs, Moulton, Wary, Winnow, Finch,
Booster and Quail; but it was stolen almost at once by
the executive vice-president, Edward DeLancy Strainge.

Young Krief had worked for several years on the
Drudge account. As you remember, *Drudge* was the all-
purpose cleanser that banished washday drudgery, made
your dishes sparkle like new, helped you bid farewell to
Blue Monday nerves, brought back life to tired eyes,
made clothes bluer than blue, ended laundry-tub wrin-
kles, contained lanolin and reduced stomach acidity.

There was a slogan about 'Don't *be* a drudge, *use*
Drudge,' and a singing commercial about never bearing
a grudge, and a lot more jazz like that.

Well, J. Algernon Krief, who had been just plain
Joe Krief until he became a junior account executive,
was put to work on the *Drudge* account, premium
division.

At first it was pretty simple. The firm printed a coupon
on the boxtop and if you saved ten of these, and if they
were all the right colour, and if you mailed them in with
two dollars in coin or stamps you received a genuine,

9

silver-plated egg-shirrer in the beautiful Carleton design, worth at least $2.49 in any retail store.

This was a mild success. It caused a flurry of coupon-trading among housewives and enough extra *Drudge* was sold to make husbands complain of a soapy taste on their butter knives. But then the makers of *Drab*, sensing competition, went *Drudge* one better.

Drab, you'll recall, was the sensational new washday miracle discovery which removed drabness from everyday life, contained an amazing new scientific suds ingredient (Radiant-5), produced rich, abundant lather, made pots and pans gleam like jewels, was kind to your skin and brought fast, fast, fast relief. I forgot to say that its gentle soothing action did wonders with laces and fine fabrics. The makers of *Drab* printed a coupon on their box which, all by itself, was good for a genuine nickel-plated olive-mincer, the kind used by many glamorous Hollywood stars. This valuable premium was rushed to your door for a mere ten cents in stamps or coins to cover packaging and mailing.

The *Drudge* people fought back fiercely. Soon the supermarket shelves were jammed with new boxes of *Drudge* in the exciting new flip-top package, which heralded the fact that no coupon at all was needed to secure a beautiful, solid chromium, hand-engraved quince-parer, designed by Raymond Loewy. One of these useful implements was actually attached to the side of each box of *Drudge*.

As a result, so much *Drudge* was sold that, in Vaughan Township alone, eighteen septic tank repairmen were able to take expensive six-week vacations at Key West.

The *Drab* company did not take this lying down. They put their next premium—a beautifully hand-tooled stainless steel nutmeg-grater—*inside* the box, mixed up with the *Drab*.

This had several advantages. For one thing there was the thrilling sense of discovery when the housewife, on shaking quantities of *Drab* into the automatic washer, suddenly spotted the nutmeg-grater churning about among the nylon panties.

Then there was the fact that the nutmeg-grater actually replaced some of the *Drab*. The company had less to make, the housewife less to get rid of. And that was how J. Algernon Krief, whose friends (alas) still called him Joe, got his great idea.

Young Krief was a man obsessed by charts, graphs, surveys in depth, door-to-door polls, motivational studies and tests. It was he, for instance, who discovered that the placing of *two* premiums, rather than one, in a box of *Drudge*, increased the angle of the sales graph by 17·4 degrees during the months of December and March.

Emboldened, Krief decided to test *three* premiums per box in eight selected cities for a period of five weeks. These premiums were: (1) A genuine zircon solitaire stickpin in a simulated 14-karat gold mounting which gave an air of success and affluence to all who wore it (for the man of the house); (2) Two giant-sized Howitzer brand bath towels, labelled *Madame* and *Monsieur* (for the housewife); and (3) An automatic Zap gun which threw a real flame fifty feet (for children).

These premiums, stuffed into enormous *Drudge* boxes, dominated the supermarkets and boosted the sale of *Drudge* by 512·3 per cent in the test cities. Even more significant, a greater number of stickpins, towels and Zap guns were sold in this way than in the normal way through retail stores.

But Krief discovered something far more significant:

though sales were up, *the actual quantity of Drudge being manufactured had dropped*. Some of the vats were only half full. The reason was simple enough: there just wasn't very much room left in the *Drudge* cartons for *Drudge*.

Then the brilliant idea came to Krief in a flash: *why bother to put any Drudge in at all?*

As I say, this idea was stolen at once by the executive vice-president, but there's no denying its revolutionary effect on the soap and detergent business.

The *Drudge* company, by firing all its research chemists statistically reduced its overhead. Housewives were delighted to find the *Drudge* packages jammed with premiums. It was like Christmas every day to buy *Drudge*. And the graphs proved that the sales of *Drudge* had increased 1013·4 per cent—even though none was being made.

Drab followed suit instantly and the entire industry swiftly swung into line. Soon other companies began boosting their own sales with premiums. In fact, even the premiums had premiums. A packaged rice firm, for example, gave away free boxes of Crackerjack which themselves contained premiums.

But it remained for the Howitzer Towel Company to reach the peak of premium giving. One of its bright young men conceived the idea of giving away free soap with each towel sold. Then as the idea caught on, packages of detergent, such as *Drudge*.

Drudge meanwhile was giving away Howitzer towels by the millions. Which meant if you wanted a Howitzer towel you bought *Drudge* and if you wanted *Drudge* you bought a Howitzer towel and everything was the same as before. Only the names were changed to confuse the innocent.

FROM *Just Add Water and Stir*

To the Rankling La

by W. E. Bowman

The account of the Rum Doodle Mountaineering Expedition is related by the leader. This description of their preliminary journey introduces the other members of the party, all of whom have been picked for their special qualifications and abilities; one member is absent, Jungle their pathfinder, who lost his way and missed the boat . . .

The voyage was uneventful. My responsibilities as leader prevented me from spending as much time as I should have liked with the others, but I was gratified to see that the *esprit-de-corps* which is so important on expeditions such as ours was uniting our party into a closely-knit community. The importance of the team spirit cannot be overestimated. As Totter once said: when you are swinging helplessly at the end of a hundred-foot rope it is important to know that the man at the other end is a *friend*. It was this spirit, more than any other single factor, which brought success, and I was happy to see it growing during the voyage.

Humour was not lacking. Wish caused much amusement by turning up for dinner one evening with a black eye which he had sustained by walking into a davit, while on the same occasion Burley exhibited a bandaged hand injured during a game of deck tennis. Burley was down most of the voyage with sea lassitude, and it was a surprise to me that he had the energy for tennis. The others kept fit, except for Prone, who alone succumbed to sea-sickness.

Wish was kept busy with his apparatus. He tested our boiling-point thermometers and was able, by averaging the results of many readings, to fix the ship's height as 153 feet above sea level. Burley said this was nonsense, but Wish pointed out that due to the earth's not being a perfect sphere, but larger at the equator than at the poles, the result was quite in accordance with known facts.

Shute took many reels of film, but by an unfortunate oversight he exposed them to daylight, so that no record exists of this portion of the journey.

Constant, to his great delight, discovered a Yogistani family on the lower deck, and spent much time with them improving his knowledge of the language. The association came to a sudden end, however, in a rather strange way. One quiet Sunday afternoon, Constant came running up the stairway in a state of terror, closely followed by a small but powerful oriental person who was waving a knife. After being rescued Constant explained that he had made a trifling error in pronunciation. He had wished to express admiration for the poetry of Yogistan. Unfortunately, the Yogistani word for poetry is identical with the word for wife, except for a sort of gurgle at the end. Being unable, in the enthusiasm of the moment, to produce this gurgle, he had deeply offended his host, with the result we had witnessed. Constant kept to his own deck for the rest of the voyage.

One day a whale was sighted on the starboard quarter. This was naturally an event of great interest to all, but particularly to myself as it enabled me to make up my mind on the very vital matter of the grouping of the assault party, to which I had given much thought. Our attack on the mountain was to be made by units of two men, who would climb together on the same rope and occupy the same tent. I considered it important that these partners be brought together as soon as possible, to enable them to rub off those rough corners which become irksome at close quarters. I had, however, been unable to reach a decision. Burley and Wish, I had decided long ago, were the ideal combination to fit into a cramped bivouac tent, one being large and the other small; and their personalities and interests were so different that there was little chance of professional jealousy or monotony arising. Shute and Jungle had each shown a lively and controversial interest in the other's special subject, and I thought it would be a pity to part them. Moreover, Shute was a Cambridge man while Jungle had been to Oxford, which would broaden the horizons of both of them. This left Constant and Prone; and I was not at all happy about these two—both having the professional manner, which might prove somewhat stifling in a small tent. But they disagreed so heartily on so many subjects that I began to be reassured, and the incident of the whale put my mind finally at rest. While we were leaning over the rail watching the creature blowing Constant said he wondered whether there was any truth in the Jonah legend. Prone said that he was surprised at such a remark from an educated man, and became so interested in the subsequent discussion that he forgot to be sea-sick. They argued heatedly for the remainder of the voyage and were quite inseparable, which was a great relief to me.

Just before we reached port I received a radio message: UNFORTUNATELY MISDIRECTED BUENOS AIRES SEND FIFTY MILLION PEONS JUNGLE.

The rail journey was uneventful. Burley was down

with heat lassitude and Prone contracted malaria. Constant remarked that it was a good thing we had a doctor with us. I am sorry to have to record that Prone took exception to this innocent remark and was quite rude to poor Constant, but the latter generously overlooked this as being due to Prone's condition. Constant went into the native portion of the train to improve his knowledge of the language, but soon afterwards a riot broke out and he thought it advisable to retire. He explained that the natives were really friendly people of imperturbable dignity and cheerfulness, but they sometimes allowed themselves to be upset by trifles. We enquired the nature of this particular trifle, but Constant said it was difficult to explain to a European. Wish spent most of the journey with a stopwatch in his hand timing the telegraph posts in order to calculate the speed of the train. This worked out at 153 miles per hour, but he thought that a certain amount of experimental error should be allowed to cover irregularities in the spacing of the posts. Burley gave him a check and found that the hand of the stopwatch had stuck. This caused much amusement.

Our arrival at Chaikhosi was a big event, both for ourselves and for the local people. Constant had arranged that the 3,000 porters should meet the train, so that no time would be lost. As we pulled in we were surprised and gratified to see that a great crowd, which stretched as far as we could see, had assembled to welcome us. When we put our heads out of the window we were greeted by a deafening cheer. Constant remarked on the friendliness of the natives, which, he said, was one of their chief characteristics.

As we stepped off the train we were met by a dignitary whom I assumed to be the local Clang, or headman.

Constant engaged him in conversation, putting on his most diplomatic air. They spoke together for several minutes, and a European onlooker might have been forgiven for concluding that they were quarrelling violently; but I told myself that this, no doubt, was the local idiom.

Finally, Constant told us that this was not the Clang at all, but the Bang, or foreman porter, and that the multitude before us were the porters he had ordered.

'If you ask me,' said Prone, 'there are a lot more than 3,000 of them.'

I was of the same opinion, but Constant said that nobody had asked Prone and he was sure the number was correct.

'Why not ask your friend?' Prone suggested.

Constant engaged the Bang in another lengthy bout, after which he told us that the man spoke an obscure dialect and did not seem fully conversant with standard Yogistani.

'Let's count 'em, then,' said Prone. 'Line 'em up ten deep.'

Constant turned again to the Bang, and after much noise and gesticulation he explained to us that there was no Yogistani phrase for ten deep and, since military training was unknown in the country, the idea of lining up was not easily conveyed to the Yogistani mind.

I told Constant we would leave him to thrash the matter out with the Bang. He said it was a good idea; we were probably making the poor fellow nervous. As we left they went to it again, holding three fingers in the air and scratching on the dusty ground with sticks.

At the post office a surprise awaited me in the form of a letter from Jungle. He had arrived by plane three days previously and had gone ahead to break the trail.

We spent a hungry and uncomfortable night in the station waiting room, for until the dispute with the Bang was settled our equipment could not be unloaded, and in the absence of Constant we dared not risk a night in the local hotel. At daybreak I walked over to the train, to find Constant and the Bang still at it. The former explained to me that the Yogistani word for three was identical with the word for thirty, except for a kind of snort in the middle. It was, of course, impossible to convey this snort by telegram, and the Bang had chosen to interpret the message as ordering 30,000 porters. The 30,000 were making a considerable noise outside, and Constant told me that they were demanding food and a month's pay. He was afraid that if we refused they would loot the train.

There was nothing for it but to meet their demands. The 30,000 were fed—at considerable trouble and expense—and three days later we were able to set off with the chosen 3,000 on our 500-mile journey. The 375 boys who completed our force were recruited on the spot. Boys are in plentiful supply in Yogistan; it appears that their mothers are glad to get rid of them.

The journey to the Rum Doodle massif was uneventful. We travelled along a series of river gorges deeply cut between precipitous ridges which rose to heights of 30,000 feet and more. Sometimes we crossed from one valley to another over passes, some over 20,000 feet above sea level, dropping again to river beds elevated to a mere 153 feet or so.

The steepness of the valleys was such that the vegetation ranged from tropical to arctic within the distance of a mile, and our botanists were in their element. I am no naturalist myself, but I tried to show an intelligent interest in the work of the others, encouraging them to come to me with their discoveries. I am indebted to them for what small knowledge I possess in this field.

The lower slopes were gay with Facetia and Persiflage, just then at their best, and the nostrils were continually assailed with the disturbing smell of Rodentia. Nostalgia, which flourishes everywhere but at home, was plentiful, as was the universal Wantonia. Higher up, dark belts of Suspicia and Melancholia gave place to the last grassy slopes below the snow line, where nothing was seen growing but an occasional solitary Excentricular, or old-fashioned Manspride.

The fauna, too, was a constant delight. The scapegoat was, of course, common, as were the platitude and the long-tailed bore. The weak-willed sloth was often met, and sometimes after dark I would catch sight of slinking shadows which Burley identified as the miserable hangdog. One afternoon Shute, in great excitement, pointed out to me a disreputable-looking creature which he said was a shaggy dog. Burley swore that it was not a shaggy dog at all but a hairy disgrace; but this may have been intended for one of his peculiar jokes. Burley's sense of humour is rather weak. He told me one day that he was being followed by a lurking suspicion, which was obviously absurd. But he is a good fellow.

We were naturally all agog to catch sight of the Atrocious Snowman, about whom so much has been written. This creature was first seen by Thudd in 1928 near the summit of Raw Deedle. He describes it as a man-like creature about seven feet tall covered with blue fur and having three ears. It emitted a thin whistle and ran off with incredible rapidity. The next reported encounter took place during the 1931 Bavarian reconnaissance expedition to Hi Hurdle. On this occasion it was seen by three members at a height of 25,000 feet. Their impressions are largely contradictory, but all agree that the thing wore trousers. In 1933 Orgrind and Stretcher found footprints on a snowslope above the Trundling La, and the following year Moodles heard grunts at 30,000 feet. Nothing further was reported until 1946, when Brewbody was fortunate enough to see the creature at close quarters. It was, he said, completely bare of either fur or hair, and resembled a human being of normal stature. It wore a loincloth and was talking to itself in Rudistani with a strong Birmingham accent. When it caught sight of Brewbody it sprang to the top of a crag and disappeared.

Such was the meagre information gleaned so far, and all were agog to add to it. The most agog among us was Wish, who may have nourished secret dreams of adding *Eoanthropus Wishi* to mankind's family tree. Wish spent much time above the snow line examining any mark which might prove to be a footprint; but although he heard grunts, whistles, sighs and gurgles, and even, on one occasion, muttering, he found no direct evidence. His enthusiasm weakened appreciably after he had spent a whole rest day tracking footprints for miles across a treacherous mountain-side, only to find that he was following a trail laid for him by a porter at Burley's instigation.

The porters were unprepossessing. Mountaineering to them was strictly business. An eight-hour day had been agreed on, for which each received *bohees* five (3¾d). Nothing on earth would persuade them to work longer than this, except money. When not on the march they squatted in groups smoking a villainous tobacco called *stunk*. Their attitude was surly in the extreme; a more desperate-looking crew can hardly be imagined. They were in such contrast to the description which Constant had given us that I was moved to mention the matter to him in a tactful way. He explained that they were used to living above the 20,000-feet line; their good qualities did not begin to appear until this height was reached. He said that they would improve as we got higher, reaching their peak of imperturbable dignity and cheerfulness at 40,000 feet. This was a great relief to me.

Their performance as porters left nothing to be desired. Although short—few were more than five feet in height—they were almost as broad as they were long, and very sturdy. Each carried a load of 1,000 pounds. One cannot praise too highly the work of the porters, without whom the expedition would have been doomed to failure.

The only one of them who was not worth his weight in *bohees* was the cook, whose name was Pong. Of all the barbarous 3,000, Pong was probably the most disreputable and the most startling in appearance. His face had a peculiarly flattened look, as though it had been pressed in by a plane surface while it was still soft. This same flattening seemed to have spread to his soul, for a more morose, unresponsive and uninspiring individual it would be impossible to imagine. His cooking was the reflection of his character. No matter what tempting delicacies he might extract from their tins the final result was an invariable and appalling dark-brown mess which had to be eaten with a strong spoon and contained the most revolting lumps. That we survived his ministrations must be considered a triumph of spirit over matter, for we suffered considerably from indigestion. All attempts to turn him out of the kitchen failed. At the least hint that we were less than delighted with his disgusting concoctions he went into a kind of frenzy and threatened us with knives.

The Bang either could or would do nothing to remove him. Perhaps they had trade union rules about it; however it was, we had to put up with Pong. No small part of our eagerness to get to grips with Rum Doodle was due to the desire, fast becoming an obsession, to get away from him. While on the march I indulged in long daydreams in which Burley and I, in a bivouac tent, cooked delicious repasts, while down below at Base Camp Pong writhes with frustration.

We passed through many villages, the inhabitants of which were invariably sullen and unfriendly, except when Constant made overtures, when they became hostile. He explained that they were not typical of the natives, being a degenerate class who, attracted by the soft living to be made below the 20,000-feet line, had become demoralised and lost their original qualities of dignity and cheerfulness. I may remark here that we came across no sign of habitation above the 20,000-feet line. This, Constant said, was because our course was away from the trade routes.

Shute was anxious to get a good film record of our progress. To do this it was necessary to start ahead of the rest so that he could set up his cameras in readiness for our coming. This simple plan proved more difficult in practice than he had anticipated. On the first three occasions he was unable to assemble his gear before we reached him, and it was as much as he could do to pack hurriedly and catch us up before evening.

Next day he made a specially early start and was not seen again until next morning, when he staggered into camp just as we were making preparations to move off. We had apparently taken different routes. This put him a day behind, for he found it necessary to make up for lost sleep. He did not catch us up until a week later, and then he went ahead and sat up all night to make sure of us. He shot the whole procession as it went past him, and everybody cheered. It was most unfortunate that on this occasion the three-dimensional camera should have developed double vision.

We were daily expecting to overhaul Jungle, although we had seen no trace of the trail which he had gone ahead to break. On the twentieth day we were overtaken by a runner with the following message: 'Captured by bandits. Send *bohees* fifty million ransom. Jungle.'

On the thirtieth day we received the following message by another runner: 'Repeat. Captured by bandits. Send *bohees* fifty million. Jungle.'

We concluded that the first messenger must have decamped with the money. After deep consideration I reasoned that I could place no reliance upon the honesty of these people, and I asked Prone, who was fully recovered from an attack of chicken-pox, to accompany the fellow. On the fortieth day Jungle reached us alone, bringing a ransom demand for *bohees* fifty million for Prone.

It was too much. I decided that the finances of the expedition could stand no more such demands. I therefore sent a trustworthy messenger with the following message: 'Sorry. Bankrupt. Contact Embassy.' On the fiftieth day Prone overtook us. Shortly after being seized by the bandits he had contracted double pneumonia aggravated by whooping cough, and had proved such a nuisance to his captors that they had turned him loose. He was a pitiable sight: unshaven, with matted hair and staring eyes. His clothes were torn to ribbons and his boots had no soles. He was suffering from mumps.

Burley, who spent most of the day drowsing in a litter carried by porters, trying to overcome his valley lassitude, awoke one afternoon screaming. He had dreamt that the expedition was starving on Rum Doodle. He produced his calculations and checked them over carefully. It was as he feared. Due no doubt to his attack of London lassitude he had forgotten to allow food for the return journey. Concentrating as he did on the one objective of placing two men on the summit of Rum Doodle, he had forgotten to bring them back again.

I saw that the crisis would tax all my resources as a leader. I said nothing to the others, but carried my burden alone for a week, searching for a way out. At last I was forced to disclose the emergency. Wish gave one look at Burley—and I like to think that even in this crisis one of us, at least, was able to spare a thought for the unhappy author—and commenced to scribble on his thumb nail.

'The solution is quite simple,' he announced. 'Dismiss all but 153 porters and 19·125 boys. The food saved will see us through.'

This was found to be correct. Constant was asked to make the necessary arrangements with the porters. The resulting uproar went on for a week, and Constant was in continual fear for his life. At last we simply could not afford to feed them for another day and we were forced to pay them what they demanded, which was too much. The one bright spot was the hope of getting rid of Pong, but for some reason this did not prove practicable. Constant said he sometimes wondered whether the Bang had a vested interest in Pong; but this, I thought, was an unduly cynical view. FROM *The Ascent of Rum Doodle*

The Night the Bed Fell

by *James Thurber*

I suppose that the high-water mark of my youth in Columbus, Ohio, was the night the bed fell on my father. It makes a better recitation (unless, as some friends of mine have said, one has heard it five or six times) than it does a piece of writing, for it is almost necessary to throw furniture around, shake doors, and bark like a dog, to lend the proper atmosphere and verisimilitude to what is admittedly a somewhat incredible tale. Still, it did take place.

It happened, then, that my father had decided to sleep in the attic one night, to be away where he could think. My mother opposed the notion strongly because, she said, the old wooden bed up there was unsafe; it was wobbly and the heavy headboard would crash down on father's head in case the bed fell, and kill him. There was no dissuading him, however, and at a quarter past ten he closed the attic door behind him and went up the narrow twisting stairs. We later heard ominous creakings as he crawled into bed. Grandfather, who usually slept in the attic bed when he was with us, had disappeared some days before. (On these occasions he was usually gone six or eight days and returned growling and out of temper, with the news that the federal Union was run by a passel of blockheads and that the Army of the Potomac didn't have any more chance than a fiddler's bitch.)

25

We had visiting us at this time a nervous first cousin of mine named Briggs Beall, who believed that he was likely to cease breathing when he was asleep. It was his feeling that if he were not awakened every hour during the night, he might die of suffocation. He had been accustomed to setting an alarm clock to ring at intervals until morning, but I persuaded him to abandon this. He slept in my room and I told him that I was such a light sleeper that if anybody quit breathing in the same room with me, I would wake instantly. He tested me the first night —which I had suspected he would—by holding his breath after my regular breathing had convinced him I was asleep. I was not asleep, however, and called to him. This seemed to allay his fears a little, but he took the precaution of putting a glass of spirits of camphor on a little table at the head of his bed. In case I didn't arouse him until he was almost gone, he said, he would sniff the camphor, a powerful reviver. Briggs was not the only member of his family who had his crotchets. Old Aunt Melissa Beall (who could whistle like a man, with two fingers in her mouth) suffered under the premonition that she was destined to die on South High Street because she had been born on South High Street and married on South High Street. Then there was Aunt Sarah Shoaf, who never went to bed at night without the fear that a burglar was going to get in and blow chloroform under her door through a tube. To avert this calamity—for she was in greater dread of anaesthetics than of losing her household goods—she always piled her money, silverware, and other valuables in a neat stack just outside her bedroom, with a note reading: 'This is all I have. Please take it and do not use your chloroform, as this is all I have.' Aunt Gracie Shoaf also had a burglar phobia, but she met it with more fortitude. She was confident that burglars had been getting into her house every night for forty years. The fact that she never missed anything was to her no proof to the contrary. She always claimed that she scared them off before they could take anything, by throwing shoes down the hallway. When she went to bed she piled, where she could get at them handily, all the shoes there were about her house. Five minutes after she had turned off the light, she would sit up in bed and say, 'Hark!' Her husband, who had learned to ignore the whole situation as long ago as 1903, would either be sound asleep or pretend to be sound asleep. In either case he would not respond to her tugging and pulling, so that presently she would arise, tiptoe to the door, open it slightly and heave a shoe down the hall in one direction, and its mate down the hall in the other direction. Some nights she threw them all, some nights only a couple of pairs.

But I am straying from the remarkable incidents that took place during the night that the bed fell on father. By midnight we were all in bed. The layout of the rooms and the disposition of their occupants is important to an understanding of what later occurred. In the front room upstairs (just under father's attic bedroom) were my mother and my brother Herman, who sometimes sang in his sleep, usually 'Marching Through Georgia' or 'Onward, Christian Soldiers'. Briggs Beall and myself were in a room adjoining this one. My brother Roy was in a room across the hall from ours. Our bull terrier, Rex, slept in the hall.

My bed was an army cot, one of those affairs which are made wide enough to sleep on comfortably only by putting up, flat with the middle section, the two sides which ordinarily hang down like sideboards of a drop-leaf table. When these sides are up, it is perilous to roll too far toward the edge, for then the cot is likely to tip completely over, bringing the whole bed down on top of one, with a tremendous banging crash. This, in fact, is precisely what happened, about two o'clock in the morning. (It was my mother who, in recalling the scene later, first referred to it as 'the night the bed fell on your father'.)

Always a deep sleeper, slow to arouse (I had lied to Briggs), I was at first unconscious of what had happened when the iron cot rolled me onto the floor and toppled over on me. It left me still warmly bundled up and unhurt, for the bed rested above me like a canopy. Hence I did not wake up, only reached the edge of consciousness and went back. The racket, however, instantly awakened my mother, in the next room, who came to the immediate conclusion that her worst dread was realised: the big wooden bed upstairs had fallen on father. She therefore screamed, 'Let's go to your poor father!' It was this shout, rather than the noise of my cot falling, that awakened Herman, in the same room as her. He thought that mother had become, for no apparent reason, hysterical. 'You're all right, Mamma!' he shouted, trying to calm her. They exchanged shout for shout for perhaps ten seconds: 'Let's go to your poor father!' and 'You're all right!' That woke up Briggs. By this time I was conscious of what was going on, in a vague way, but did not yet realise that I was under my bed instead of on it. Briggs, awakening in the midst of loud shouts of fear and apprehension, came to the quick conclusion that he was suffocating and that we were all trying to 'bring him out'. With a low moan, he grasped the glass of camphor at the head of his bed and instead of sniffing it poured it over himself. The room reeked of camphor. 'Ugf, ahfg,' choked Briggs, like a drowning man, for he had almost succeeded in stopping his breath under the deluge of pungent spirits. He leaped out of bed and groped toward the open window, but he came up against one that was closed. With his hand, he beat out the glass, and I could hear it crash and tinkle on the alleyway below. It was at this juncture that I, in trying to get up, had the uncanny sensation of feeling my bed above me! Foggy with sleep, I now suspected, in my turn, that the whole uproar was being made in a frantic endeavour to extricate me from what must be an unheard-of and perilous situation. 'Get me out of this!' I bawled. 'Get me out!' I think I had the nightmarish belief that I was entombed in a mine. 'Gugh,' gasped Briggs, floundering in his camphor.

By this time my mother, still shouting, pursued by Herman, still shouting, was trying to open the door to the attic, in order to go up and get my father's body out of the wreckage. The door was stuck, however, and wouldn't yield, her frantic pulls on it only added to the general banging and confusion. Roy and the dog were now up, the one shouting questions, the other barking.

Father, farthest away and soundest sleeper of all, had by this time been awakened by the battering on the attic door. He decided that the house was on fire. 'I'm coming, I'm coming!' he wailed in a slow, sleepy voice— it took him many minutes to regain full consciousness. My mother, still believing he was caught under the bed, detected in his 'I'm coming!' the mournful, resigned note of one who is preparing to meet his Maker. 'He's dying!' she shouted.

'I'm all right!' Briggs yelled to reassure her. 'I'm all right!' He still believed that it was his own closeness to death that was worrying mother. I found at last the light switch in my room, unlocked the door, and Briggs and I joined the others at the attic door. The dog, who never did like Briggs, jumped for him—assuming that he was the culprit in whatever was going on—and Roy had to throw Rex and hold him. We could hear father crawling out of bed upstairs. Roy pulled the attic door open with a mighty jerk, and father came down the stairs, sleepy and irritable but safe and sound. My mother began to weep when she saw him. Rex began to howl. 'What in the name of God is going on here?' asked father.

The situation was finally put together like a gigantic jig-saw puzzle. Father caught a cold from prowling around in his bare feet but there were no other bad results. 'I'm glad,' said mother, who always looked on the bright side of things, 'that your grandfather wasn't here.'

FROM *My Life and Hard Times*

Car Episode

by Barry Crump

An unregistered Model A truck with a boiling radiator
chuttered round the corner and stopped with a cloud of
white steam geysering into the early morning darkness
from somewhere under the bonnet. Jack struck a match
in front of a glassless alarm-clock that hung on a piece of
wire from the dashboard. Then he climbed out and got
a stick off the back to dip the petrol-tank with.

Three o'clock in the morning and out of gas. If he
didn't get his bomb out of this town, whatever it was,
and into the country by daylight he'd get run in and
they'd probably get in touch with his old man, and
there'd be a hell of a stink. Especially when they found
out about him getting the sack from the garage.

In another four years, eight months, three weeks and
two days he would have been a certified mechanic, if he'd
checked the chocks under the new Austin that tipped off
the lubrication hoist yesterday. It seemed like a year
since he'd signed for his pay and driven south without
knowing where he was going. Or caring much either.
Now he didn't even know where he was. And there was
no going back after that letter he'd posted home as he
passed through Warkworth.

He walked along to a car that was parked on the road-
side, lifting a couple of quart milk bottles off a gatepost
on the way. The cap on the tank wasn't locked and he

was looking in the boot for a siphon-hose when a prowl car slid round the bend and pinned him with a spotlight to the scene of his first crime. He kicked the milk bottles on to the grass verge with the side of his foot as the black car stopped beside him. The light shifted from his face to the hand in which he still clutched the petrol-cap, and he saw that there were two black uniforms in the car.

Well now, said the one with the light, getting out and flashing a notebook. What've we got here? That your car lad?

Not exactly. I was just having a look at it.

A look, eh? A look into the petrol-tank. What's your name?

Jack Lilburn.

Got your driver's licence with you?

No.

Where do you live?

Whangarei—I'm looking for a job.

Unemployed, eh? And whose car is this?

I suppose it belongs to the people in this house.

Well, let's just go and make sure, shall we? Come on Blake.

The other uniform got out of the car and Jack walked between them to see the car owner. At their second knock somebody moved inside the house and a light went on over their heads. The door opened and a tall, thin, whiskery man of about forty said: What the hell?

Then he saw the uniforms and Jack's frightened face. He looked at Jack.

That your green Chevrolet, registered number eight five eight three seven three, parked outside here? asked the first policeman.

Yeah, why? said the thin man slowly, still looking at Jack.

We caught this character in the act of interfering with it. He had the boot open and the cap of the petrol-tank in his hand. Now if you would just come along to the station with us . . .

Hell, what a time of the day to run out of gas! said the thin man to Jack, ignoring the policeman. Hang on a tick and I'll give you a hand. There's usually a tin lying around in the washhouse here somewhere.

I'm afraid I'll have to ask you to come down to head-quarters with us, sir, said the policeman, looking a bit annoyed. We're placing this chap under arrest, and we'll need your statement.

What! said the thin man. Don't you think he's had enough trouble for one night? First the poor sod runs out of juice, and then you blokes have to pounce on him. As a matter of fact I told young Bill here a couple of weeks ago that any time he wanted a gallon . . .

I wouldn't advise that now, sir, interrupted the police-man, holding up his hand. We won't keep you long. There's been too much of this sort of thing going on around here lately. You'll get no thanks for trying to help these types. They've got no respect for anyone's . . .

Now just you hang on there a minute, mate! said the thin man, coming out on to the porch and standing close up to the policeman, who stepped back and stood on the second step, looking up at him. You can't come round here waking a man up in the early hours of the morning and then practically calling him a liar to his face. By strike, there'll be trouble over this, believe me! You blokes have overstepped the mark this time, and I'm just the wrong bloke to do it to. One more insult and I'll come down to the station all right. And I'll have Harvey Wilson himself with me, and you know what that means!

We're only doing our job, sir. The policeman spoke

much less aggressively and avoided the thin man's eyes. It's our duty to investigate any suspicious circumstances.

Well, you've investigated them, haven't you? Young Bill here's been a friend of the family for I don't know how long. Trouble with you blokes is you won't admit when you've made a blue.

Since you refuse to co-operate with us we'll consider the matter closed for the time being—but if we catch this character round the streets at this hour again I'll remember this.

So! said the thin man. It's threats now, is it? I'm not sure that I won't see Harvey Wilson first thing in the morning, after all. I'm not standing for any more of this sort of nonsense!

The policemen left, and on turning from watching them climb the steps to the gate, Jack saw that the thin man was grinning delightedly.

Er—thanks very much . . . he began embarrassedly.

Ar, forget it, said the thin man, still grinning. I wouldn't see a man in the cart for a lousy couple of gallons of petrol. He sat on the top step and began rolling a cigarette. Jack noticed for the first time that he was fully dressed.

Y'know, it reminds me of the time a mate and I ran out of gas fair slap in the middle of Hamilton. Ten o'clock at night, and we never had a cracker. Heading for a job at Kawerau, we were. My mate said he'd take the tin and see if he could half-inch a gallon or two, and I went with him to keep an eye on things. Well, the first chariot my mate claps his eye on is a taxi standing outside a coffee shop, and he bowls up, lifts the cap and shoves his pipe into this bloke's tank, saying we had more chance of getting away with it if we swiped the stuff publicly. Just when we looked like pulling it off a bloke comes out of

34

this coffee joint and says: 'Hey, who told you you could take that petrol out of there?'

'Who the hell do you think?' says my mate. 'The owner of the bloomin' car, of course!'

'Okay,' says this bloke. 'Don't get your back up, mate. I only drive for him. Never know what to expect from old Barney.'

'Anyone would think we were swipin' the blasted stuff, the way you come up and beller at a man!' says my mate. 'Here, hang on to this tin and I'll get ready to pull the hose out. Don't want to waste any. One of Barney's mates has run out of gas four mile out!'

And this bloke gives us a hand to milk his boss's car. My mate reckoned he'd never laughed so much since his brother's pig-dogs got loose and followed him into the Waitawheta dance hall . . .!

Now, let's see about this petrol of yours.

He found a hose and a two-gallon tin and they went up to the car. Waiting for the tin to fill, the thin man said:

Where you heading, son?

South.

Yeah? Any particular place?

No. Just south.

On your own? The thin man seemed interested.

Yeah, I'll have a look round for a job when I get down Taihape way.

You'll do all right down there, said the thin man. There's mustering, and shearing gangs this time of year. Fencing and scrub-cutting, packing, logging—any amount of jobs going. Never tell them you can't do a thing. Get stuck in and have a go. By the time they find out you've never done it before, you're doing it.

While they were pouring the third tin of petrol into

Jack's little truck, the thin man, who'd been silent for a few minutes, suddenly said: You got enough room for a passenger for down the line, mate?

Too right! said Jack. Far as you like.

Right, I'll just nick down and grab a few hunks of gear and be right with you.

He returned in a few minutes with a shotgun and a full pack, threw them on the back of Jack's truck and stuck his hand across the bonnet.

By the way, my name's Sam Cash.

Mine's Jack Lilburn. Pleased to meet you.

Same here.

As they swung out to drive off, Jack said: Hey, what about your car?

I haven't got one, said Sam, grinning. I think that's the bloke next door's. Proper ratbag of a joker he is, too.

They laughed for a half a mile.

By the way, Sam, who's Harvey Wilson?

I think he was someone in a book I read once, replied Sam. They laughed for another half-mile.

Good thing those johns didn't get a decent look at this bomb of yours, said Sam, folding a wad of paper to jam the window up. We'd have had a job talking our way out of this little lot.

FROM *Hang on a Minute, Mate*

The Arrival
of Blackman's Warbler

by A. A. Milne

I am become an Authority on Birds. It happened in this
way.

The other day we heard the Cuckoo in Hampshire.
(The next morning the papers announced that the
Cuckoo had been heard in Devonshire—possibly a different one, but in no way superior to ours except in the
matter of its press agent.) Well, everybody in the house
said, 'Did you hear the Cuckoo?' to everybody else, until
I began to get rather tired of it; and, having told everybody several times that I *had* heard it, I tried to make the
conversation more interesting. So, after my tenth 'Yes',
I added quite casually:

'But I haven't heard the Tufted Pipit yet. It's funny
why it should be so late this year.'

'Is that the same as the Tree Pipit?' said my hostess,
who seemed to know more about birds than I had hoped.

'Oh, no,' I said quickly.

'What's the difference exactly?'

'Well, one is tufted,' I said, doing my best, 'and the
other—er—climbs trees.'

'Oh, I see.'

'And of course the eggs are more speckled,' I added,
gradually acquiring confidence.

'I often wish I knew more about birds,' she said regretfully. 'You must tell us something about them now we've got you here.'

And all this because of one miserable Cuckoo!

'By all means,' I said, wondering how long it would take to get a book about birds down from London.

However, it was easier than I thought. We had tea in the garden that afternoon, and a bird of some kind struck up in the plane tree.

'There, now,' said my hostess, 'what's that?'

I listened with my head on one side. The bird said it again.

'That's the Lesser Bunting,' I said hopefully.

'The Lesser Bunting,' said an earnest-looking girl; 'I shall always remember that.'

I hoped she wouldn't, but I could hardly say so. Fortunately the bird lesser-bunted again, and I seized the opportunity of playing for safety.

'Or is it the Sardinian White-throat?' I wondered. 'They have very much the same note during the breeding season. But of course the eggs are more speckled,' I added casually.

And so on for the rest of the evening. You see how easy it is.

However, the next afternoon a more unfortunate occurrence occurred. A real Bird Authority came to tea. As soon as the information leaked out, I sent up a hasty prayer for bird-silence until we had got him safely out of the place; but it was not granted. Our feathered songster in the plane tree broke into his little piece.

'There,' said my hostess—'there's that bird again.' She turned to me. 'What did you say it was?'

I hoped that the Authority would speak first, and that the others would then accept my assurance that they had misunderstood me the day before; but he was entangled at that moment in a watercress sandwich, the loose ends of which were still waiting to be tucked away.

I looked anxiously at the girl who had promised to remember, in case she wanted to say something, but she also was silent. Everybody was silent except that miserable bird.

Well, I had to have another go at it. 'Blackman's Warbler,' I said firmly.

'Oh, yes,' said my hostess.

'Blackman's Warbler; I shall always remember that,' lied the earnest-looking girl.

The Authority, who was free by this time, looked at me indignantly.

'Nonsense,' he said; 'it's the Chiff-chaff.'

Everybody else looked at me reproachfully. I was about to say that 'Blackman's Warbler' was the local name for the Chiff-chaff in our part of Somerset, when the Authority spoke again.

'The Chiff-chaff,' he said to our hostess with an insufferable air of knowledge.

I wasn't going to stand that.

'So *I* thought when I heard it first,' I said, giving him a gentle smile.

It was now the Authority's turn to get the reproachful looks.

'Are they very much alike?' my hostess asked me, much impressed.

'Very much. Blackman's Warbler is often mistaken for the Chiff-chaff, even by so-called experts'—and I turned to the Authority and added, 'Have another sandwich, won't you?—particularly so, of course, during the breeding season. It is true that the eggs are more speckled, but—'

39

'Bless my soul,' said the Authority, but it was easy to see that he was shaken, 'I should think I know a Chiff-chaff when I hear one.'

'Ah, but do you know a Blackman's Warbler? One doesn't often hear them in this country. Now in Algiers—'

The bird said 'Chiff-chaff' again with an almost indecent plainness of speech.

'There you are!' I said triumphantly. 'Listen,' and I held up a finger. 'You notice the difference? *Obviously* a Blackman's Warbler.'

Everybody looked at the Authority. He was wondering how long it would take to get a book about birds down from London, and deciding that it couldn't be done that afternoon. Meanwhile he did not dare repudiate me. For all he had caught of our mumbled introduction I might have been Blackman himself.

'Possibly you're right,' he said reluctantly.

Another bird said 'Chiff-chaff' from another tree and I thought it wise to be generous. 'There,' I said, 'now that *was* a Chiff-chaff.'

The earnest-looking girl remarked (silly creature) that it sounded just like the other one, but nobody took any notice of her. They were all busy admiring me.

Of course I mustn't meet the Authority again, because you may be pretty sure that when he got back to his books he looked up Blackman's Warbler and found that there was no such animal. But if you mix in the right society, and only see the wrong people once, it is really quite easy to be an authority on birds—or, I imagine, on anything else.   FROM *Those Were the Days*

The Standard of Living

by Dorothy Parker

Annabel and Midge came out of the tea room with the arrogant slow gait of the leisured, for their Saturday afternoon stretched ahead of them. They had lunched, as was their wont, on sugar, starches, oils and butter-fats. Usually they ate sandwiches of spongy new white bread greased with butter and mayonnaise; they ate thick wedges of cake lying wet beneath ice cream and whipped cream and melted chocolate gritty with nuts. As alternates, they ate patties, sweating beads of inferior oil, containing bits of bland meat bogged in pale, stiffening sauce; they ate pastries, limber under rigid icing, filled with an indeterminate yellow sweet stuff, not still solid, not yet liquid, like salve that has been left in the sun. They chose no other sort of food, nor did they consider it. And their skin was like the petals of wood anemones, and their bellies were as flat and their flanks as lean as those of young Indian braves.

Annabel and Midge had been best friends almost from the day that Midge had found a job as stenographer with the firm that employed Annabel. By now, Annabel, two years longer in the stenographic department, had worked up to the wages of eighteen dollars and fifty cents a week; Midge was still at sixteen dollars. Each girl lived at home with her family and paid half her salary to its support.

The girls sat side by side at their desks, they lunched

together every noon, together they set out for home at
the end of the day's work. Many of their evenings and
most of their Sundays were passed in each other's company. Often they were joined by two young men, but there
was no steadiness to any such quartet; the two young men
would give place, unlamented, to two other young men,
and lament would have been inappropriate, really, since
the newcomers were scarcely distinguishable from their
predecessors. Invariably the girls spent the fine idle hours
of their hot-weather Saturday afternoons together. Constant use had not worn ragged the fabric of their friendship.

They looked alike, though the resemblance did not lie
in their features. It was in the shape of their bodies, their
movements, their style and their adornments. Annabel
and Midge did, and completely, all that young office
workers are besought not to do. They painted their lips
and their nails, they darkened their lashes and lightened
their hair, and scent seemed to shimmer from them. They
wore thin, bright dresses, tight over their breasts and
high on their legs, and tilted slippers, fancifully strapped.
They looked conspicuous and cheap and charming.

Now, as they walked across to Fifth Avenue with their
skirts swirled by the hot wind, they received audible admiration. Young men grouped lethargically about news-
stands awarded them murmurs, exclamations, even—the
ultimate tribute—whistles. Annabel and Midge passed
without the condescension of hurrying their pace; they
held their heads higher and set their feet with exquisite
precision, as if they stepped over the necks of peasants.

Always the girls went to walk on Fifth Avenue on their
free afternoons, for it was the ideal ground for their
favourite game. The game could be played anywhere,
and, indeed, was, but the great shop windows stimulated
the two players to their best form.

Annabel had invented the game; or rather she had evolved it from an old one. Basically, it was no more than the ancient sport of what-would-you-do-if-you-had-a-million-dollars? But Annabel had drawn a new set of rules for it, had narrowed it, pointed it, made it stricter. Like all games, it was the more absorbing for being more difficult.

Annabel's version went like this: You must suppose that somebody dies and leaves you a million dollars, cool. But there is a condition to the bequest. It is stated in the will that you must spend every nickel of the money on yourself.

There lay the hazard of the game. If, when playing it, you forgot, and listed among your expenditures the rental of a new apartment for your family, for example, you lost your turn to the other player. It was astonishing how many—and some of them among the experts, too—would forfeit all their innings by such slips.

It was essential, of course, that it be played in passionate seriousness. Each purchase must be carefully considered and, if necessary, supported by argument. There was no zest to playing wildly. Once Annabel had introduced the game to Sylvia, another girl who worked in the office. She explained the rules to Sylvia and then offered her the gambit, 'What would be the first thing you'd do?' Sylvia had not shown the decency of even a second of hesitation. 'Well,' she said, 'the first thing I'd do, I'd go out and hire somebody to shoot Mrs Gary Cooper, and then . . .' So it is to be seen that she was no fun.

But Annabel and Midge were surely born to be comrades, for Midge played the game like a master from the moment she learned it. It was she who added the touches that made the whole thing cosier. According to Midge's innovations, the eccentric who died and left you the money was not anybody you loved, or for the matter of

that, anybody you even knew. It was somebody who had
seen you somewhere and had thought, 'That girl ought
to have lots of nice things. I'm going to leave her a
million dollars when I die.' And the death was to be
neither untimely nor painful. Your benefactor, full of
years and comfortably ready to depart, was to slip softly
away during sleep and go right to heaven. These em-
broideries permitted Annabel and Midge to play their
game in the luxury of peaceful consciences.

Midge played with a seriousness that was not only
proper but extreme. The single strain on the girls' friendship had followed an announcement once made by Annabel that the first thing she would buy with her million
dollars would be a silver-fox coat. It was as if she had
struck Midge across the mouth. When Midge recovered
her breath, she cried that she couldn't imagine how
Annabel could do such a thing—silver-fox coats were
common! Annabel defended her taste with the retort that
they were not common, either. Midge then said that they
were so. She added that everybody had a silver-fox coat.
She went on, with perhaps a slight toss of head, to declare
that she herself wouldn't be caught dead in silver fox.

For the next few days, though the girls saw each other
as constantly, their conversation was careful and infrequent, and they did not once play their game. Then one
morning, as soon as Annabel entered the office, she came
to Midge, and said that she had changed her mind. She
would not buy a silver-fox coat with any part of her
million dollars. Immediately on receiving the legacy, she
would select a coat of mink.

Midge smiled and her eyes shone. 'I think,' she said,
'you're doing absolutely the right thing.'

Now, as they walked along Fifth Avenue, they played
the game anew. It was one of those days with which

September is repeatedly cursed; hot and glaring, with slivers of dust in the wind. People drooped and shambled, but the girls carried themselves tall and walked in a straight line, as befitted young heiresses on their afternoon promenade. There was no longer need for them to start the game at its formal opening. Annabel went direct to the heart of it.

'All right,' she said. 'So you've got this million dollars. So what would be the first thing you'd do?'

'Well, the first thing I'd do,' Midge said, 'I'd get a mink coat.' But she said it mechanically, as if she were giving the memorized answer to an expected question.

'Yes,' Annabel said, 'I think you ought to. The terribly dark kind of mink.' But she, too, spoke as if by rote. It was too hot; fur, no matter how dark and sleek and supple, was horrid to the thoughts.

They stepped along in silence for a while. Then Midge's eye was caught by a shop window. Cool, lovely gleamings were there set off by chaste and elegant darkness.

'No,' Midge said, 'I take it back. I wouldn't get a mink coat the first thing. Know what I'd do? I'd get a string of pearls. Real pearls.'

Annabel's eyes turned to follow Midge's.

'Yes,' she said slowly. 'I think that's a kind of a good idea. And it would make sense, too. Because you can wear pearls with anything.'

Together they went over to the shop window and stood pressed against it. It contained but one object—a double row of great, even pearls clasped by a deep emerald around a little pink velvet throat.

'What do you suppose they cost?' Annabel said.

'Gee, I don't know,' Midge said. 'Plenty, I guess.'

'Like a thousand dollars?' Annabel said.

'Oh, I guess like more,' Midge said. 'On account of the emerald.'

'Well, like ten thousand dollars?' Annabel said.

'Gee, I wouldn't even know,' Midge said.

The devil nudged Annabel in the ribs. 'Dare you to go in and price them,' she said.

'Like fun!' Midge said.

'Dare you,' Annabel said.

'Why, a store like this wouldn't even be open this afternoon,' Midge said.

'Yes, it is so, too,' Annabel said. 'People just came out. And there's a doorman on. Dare you.'

'Well,' Midge said. 'But you've got to come too.'

They tendered thanks, icily, to the doorman for ushering them into the shop. It was cool and quiet, a broad, gracious room with panelled walls and soft carpet. But the girls wore expressions of bitter disdain, as if they stood in a sty.

A slim, immaculate clerk came to them and bowed. His neat face showed no astonishment at their appearance.

'Good afternoon,' he said. He implied that he would never forget it if they would grant him the favour of accepting his soft-spoken greeting.

'Good afternoon,' Annabel and Midge said together, and in like freezing accents.

'Is there something—?' the clerk said.

'Oh, we're just looking,' Annabel said. It was as if she flung the words down from a dais.

The clerk bowed.

'My friend and myself merely happened to be passing,' Midge said, and stopped, seeming to listen to the phrase. 'My friend here and myself,' she went on, 'merely happened to be wondering how much are those pearls you've got in your window.'

'Ah, yes,' the clerk said. 'The double rope. That is two hundred and fifty thousand dollars, Madam.'

'I see,' Midge said.

The clerk bowed. 'An exceptionally beautiful necklace,' he said. 'Would you care to look at it?'

'No, thank you,' Annabel said.

'My friend and myself merely happened to be passing,' Midge said.

They turned to go; to go, from their manner, where the tumbrel awaited them. The clerk sprang ahead and opened the door. He bowed as they swept by him.

The girls went on along the Avenue and disdain was still on their faces.

'Honestly!' Annabel said. 'Can you imagine a thing like that?'

'Two hundred and fifty thousand dollars!' Midge said. 'That's a quarter of a million dollars right there!'

'He's got his nerve!' Annabel said.

They walked on. Slowly the disdain went, slowly and completely as if drained from them, and with it went the regal carriage and tread. Their shoulders dropped and they dragged their feet; they bumped against each other, without notice or apology, and caromed away again. They were silent and their eyes were cloudy.

Suddenly Midge straightened her back, flung her head high, and spoke, clear and strong.

'Listen, Annabel,' she said. 'Look. Suppose there was this terribly rich person, see? You don't know this person, but this person has seen you somewhere and wants to do something for you. Well, it's a terribly old person, see? And so this person dies, just like going to sleep, and leaves you ten million dollars. Now, what would be the first thing you'd do?'

FROM *The Collected Dorothy Parker*

'Q.' A Psychic Pstory
of the Psupernatural

by Stephen Leacock

I cannot expect that any of my readers will believe the story which I am about to narrate. Looking back upon it, I scarcely believe it myself. Yet my narrative is so extraordinary and throws such light upon the nature of our communications with beings of another world, that I feel I am not entitled to withhold it from the public.

I had gone over to visit Annerly at his rooms. It was Saturday, October 31. I remember the date so precisely because it was my pay day, and I had received six sovereigns and ten shillings. I remember the sum so exactly because I had put the money into my pocket, and I remember into which pocket I had put it because I had no money in any other pocket. My mind is perfectly clear on all these points.

Annerly and I sat smoking for some time.

Then quite suddenly—

'Do you believe in the supernatural?' he asked.

I started as if I had been struck.

At the moment when Annerly spoke of the supernatural I had been thinking of something entirely different. The fact that he should speak of it at the very instant when I was thinking of something else, struck me as at least a very singular coincidence.

For a moment I could only stare.

'What I mean is,' said Annerly, 'do you believe in phantasms of the dead?'

'Phantasms?' I repeated.

'Yes, phantasms, or if you prefer the word, phano-grams, or say if you will phonogrammatical manifesta-tions, or more simply psychophantasmal phenomena?'

I looked at Annerly with a keener sense of interest than I had ever felt in him before. I felt that he was about to deal with events and experiences of which in the two or three months that I had known him he had never seen fit to speak.

I wondered now that it had never occurred to me that a man whose hair at fifty-five was already streaked with grey must have passed through some terrible ordeal.

Presently Annerly spoke again.

'Last night I saw Q,' he said.

'Good heavens!' I ejaculated. I did not in the least know who Q was, but it struck me with a thrill of in-describable terror that Annerly had seen Q. In my own quiet and measured existence such a thing had never happened.

'Yes,' said Annerly, 'I saw Q as plainly as if he were standing here. But perhaps I had better tell you some-thing of my past relationship with Q, and you will under-stand exactly what the present situation is.'

Annerly seated himself in a chair on the other side of the fire from me, lighted a pipe and continued.

'When first I knew Q he lived not very far from a small town in the south of England, which I will call X, and was betrothed to a beautiful and accomplished girl whom I will name M.'

Annerly had hardly begun to speak before I found myself listening with riveted attention. I realised that it was no ordinary experience that he was about to narrate. I more than suspected that Q and M were not the real names of his unfortunate acquaintances, but were in reality two letters of the alphabet selected almost at random to disguise the names of his friends. I was still pondering over the ingenuity of the thing when Annerly went on:

'When Q and I first became friends, he had a favourite dog, which, if necessary, I might name Z, and which followed him in and out of X on his daily walk.'

'In and out of X,' I repeated in astonishment.

'Yes,' said Annerly, 'in and out.'

My senses were now fully alert. That Z should have followed Q out of X, I could readily understand, but that he should first have followed him in seemed to pass the bounds of comprehension.

'Well,' said Annerly, 'Q and Miss M were to be married. Everything was arranged. The wedding was to take place on the last day of the year. Exactly six months and four days before the appointed day (I remember the date because the coincidence struck me as peculiar at the time) Q came to me late in the evening in great distress. He had just had, he said, a premonition of his own death. That evening, while sitting with Miss M on the verandah of her house, he had distinctly seen a projection of the dog R pass along the road.'

'Stop a moment,' I said. 'Did you not say that the dog's name was Z?'

Annerly frowned slightly.

'Quite so,' he replied. 'Z, or more correctly Z R, since Q was in the habit, perhaps from motives of affection, of calling him R as well as Z. Well, then, the projection, or phanogram, of the dog passed in front of them so plainly that Miss M swore that she could have believed that it was the dog himself. Opposite the house the phantasm stopped for a moment and wagged its tail. Then it passed on, and quite suddenly disappeared around the corner of a stone wall, as if hidden by the bricks. What made the thing still more mysterious was that Miss M's mother, who is partially blind, had only partially seen the dog.'

Annerly paused a moment. Then he went on:

'This singular occurrence was interpreted by Q, no doubt correctly, to indicate his own approaching death. I did what I could to remove this feeling, but it was impossible to do so, and he presently wrung my hand and left me, firmly convinced that he would not live till morning.'

'Good heavens!' I exclaimed, 'and he died that night?'

'No, he did not,' said Annerly quietly, 'that is the inexplicable part of it.'

'Tell me about it,' I said.

'He rose that morning as usual, dressed himself with his customary care, omitting none of his clothes, and walked down to his office at the usual hour. He told me afterwards that he remembered the circumstances so clearly from the fact that he had gone to the office by the usual route instead of taking any other direction.'

'Stop a moment,' I said. 'Did anything unusual happen to mark that particular day?'

'I anticipated that you would ask that question,' said Annerly, 'but as far as I can gather, absolutely nothing happened. Q returned from his work, and ate his dinner apparently much as usual, and presently went to bed complaining of a slight feeling of drowsiness, but nothing more. His stepmother, with whom he lived, said afterwards that she could hear the sound of his breathing quite distinctly during the night.'

'And did he die that night?' I asked, breathless with excitement.

'No,' said Annerly, 'he did not. He rose next morning feeling about as before except that the sense of drowsiness had apparently passed, and that the sound of his breathing was no longer audible.'

Annerly again fell into silence. Anxious as I was to hear the rest of his astounding narrative, I did not like to press him with questions. The fact that our relations had hitherto been only of a formal character, and that this was the first occasion on which he had invited me to visit him at his rooms, prevented me from assuming too great an intimacy.

'Well,' he continued, 'Q went to his office each day after that with absolute regularity. As far as I can gather there was nothing either in his surroundings or his conduct to indicate that any peculiar fate was impending over him. He saw Miss M regularly, and the time fixed for their marriage drew nearer each day.'

'Each day?' I repeated in astonishment.

'Yes,' said Annerly, 'every day. For some time before his marriage I saw but little of him. But two weeks before that event was due to happen, I passed Q one day in the street. He seemed for a moment about to stop, then he raised his hat, smiled and passed on.'

'One moment,' I said, 'if you will allow me a question that seems of importance—did he pass on and then smile and raise his hat, or did he smile into his hat, raise it, and then pass on afterwards?'

'Your question is quite justified,' said Annerly, 'though I think I can answer with perfect accuracy that he first smiled, then stopped smiling and raised his hat, and then stopped raising his hat and passed on.'

'However,' he continued, 'the essential fact is this: on the day appointed for the wedding, Q and Miss M were duly married.'

'Impossible!' I gasped; 'duly married, both of them?'

'Yes,' said Annerly, 'both at the same time. After the wedding Mr and Mrs Q—'

'Mr and Mrs Q,' I repeated in perplexity.

'Yes,' he answered, 'Mr and Mrs Q—for after the wedding Miss M took the name of Q—left England and went out to Australia, where they were to reside.'

'Stop one moment,' I said, 'and let me be quite clear— in going out to settle in Australia it was their intention to reside there?'

'Yes,' said Annerly, 'that at any rate was generally understood. I myself saw them off on the steamer, and shook hands with Q, standing at the same time quite close to him.'

'Well,' I said, 'and since the two Q's, as I suppose one might almost call them, went to Australia, have you heard anything from them?'

'That,' replied Annerly, 'is a matter that has shown the same singularity as the rest of my experience. It is now four years since Q and his wife went to Australia. At first I heard from him quite regularly, and received two letters each month. Presently I only received one letter every two months, and later two letters every six months, and then only one letter every twelve months. Then until last night I heard nothing whatever of Q for a year and a half.'

I was now on the tiptoe of expectancy.

'Last night,' said Annerly very quietly, 'Q appeared in this room, or rather, a phantasm or psychic manifestation of him. He seemed in great distress, made gestures which I could not understand, and kept turning his trouser pockets inside out. I was too spellbound to question him, and tried in vain to divine his meaning. Presently the phantasm seized a pencil from the table, and wrote the words, "Two sovereigns, tomorrow night, urgent." '

Annerly was again silent. I sat in deep thought. 'How do you interpret the meaning which Q's phanogram meant to convey?'

'I think,' he announced, 'it means this. Q, who is evidently dead, meant to visualise that fact, meant, so to speak, to deatomise the idea that he was demonetised, and that he wanted two sovereigns tonight.'

'And how,' I asked, amazed at Annerly's instinctive penetration into the mysteries of the psychic world, 'how do you intend to get it to him?'

'I intend,' he announced, 'to try a bold, a daring experiment, which, if it succeeds, will bring us into immediate connection with the world of spirits. My plan is to leave two sovereigns here upon the edge of the table during the night. If they are gone in the morning, I shall know that Q has contrived to de-astralise himself, and has taken the sovereigns. The only question is, do you happen to have two sovereigns? I myself, unfortunately, have nothing but small change about me.'

Here was a piece of rare good fortune, the coincidence of which seemed to add another link to the chain of circumstance. As it happened I had with me the six sovereigns which I had just drawn as my week's pay.

'Luckily,' I said, 'I am able to arrange that. I happen to have money with me.' And I took two sovereigns from my pocket.

Annerly was delighted at our good luck. Our preparations for the experiment were soon made.

We placed the table in the middle of the room in such a way that there could be no fear of contact or collision with any of the furniture. The chairs were carefully set against the wall, and so placed that no two of them occupied the same place as any other two, while the pictures and ornaments about the room were left entirely undisturbed. We were careful not to remove any of the wallpaper from the wall, nor to detach any of the window-panes from the window. When all was ready the two sovereigns were laid side by side upon the table, with their heads up in such a way that the lower sides or tails were supported by only the table itself. We then extinguished the light. I said 'Good night' to Annerly, and groped my way out into the dark, feverish with excitement.

My readers may well imagine my state of eagerness to know the result of the experiment. I could scarcely sleep for anxiety to know the issue. I had, of course, every faith in the completeness of our preparations, but was not without misgivings that the experiment might fail, as my own mental temperament and disposition might not be of the precise kind needed for the success of these experiments.

On this score, however, I need have had no alarm. The event showed that my mind was a media, or if the word is better, a transparency, of the very first order for psychic work of this character.

In the morning Annerly came rushing over to my lodgings, his face beaming with excitement.

'Glorious, glorious,' he almost shouted, 'we have succeeded! The sovereigns are gone. We are in direct monetary communication with Q.'

I need not dwell on the exquisite thrill of happiness which went through me. All that day and all the following day, the sense that I was in communication with Q was ever present with me.

My only hope was that an opportunity might offer for the renewal of our inter-communication with the spirit world.

The following night my wishes were gratified. Late in the evening Annerly called me up on the telephone.

'Come over at once to my lodgings,' he said. 'Q's phanogram is communicating with us.'

I hastened over, and arrived almost breathless.

'Q has been here again,' said Annerly, 'and appeared in the same distress as before. A projection of him stood in the room, and kept writing with its finger on the table. I could distinguish the word "sovereigns", but nothing more.'

'Do you not suppose,' I said, 'that Q for some reason which we cannot fathom, wishes us to again leave two sovereigns for him?'

'By Jove!' said Annerly enthusiastically, 'I believe you've hit it. At any rate, let us try; we can but fail.'

That night we placed again two of my sovereigns on the table, and arranged the furniture with the same scrupulous care as before.

Still somewhat doubtful of my own psychic fitness for the work in which I was engaged, I endeavoured to keep my mind so poised as to readily offer a mark for any astral disturbance that might be about. The result showed that it had offered just such a mark. Our experiment succeeded completely. The two coins had vanished in the morning.

For nearly two months we continued our experiments on these lines. At times Annerly himself, so he told me, would leave money, often considerable sums, within reach of the phantasm, which never failed to remove them during the night. But Annerly, being a man of strict honour, never carried on these experiments alone except when it proved impossible to communicate with me in time for me to come.

At other times he would call me up with the simple message, 'Q is here,' or would send me a telegram, or a written note saying, 'Q needs money; bring any that you have, but no more.'

On my own part, I was extremely anxious to bring our experiments prominently before the public, or to interest the Society for Psychic Research, and similar bodies, in the daring transit which we had effected between the world of sentience and the psycho-astric, or pseudo-ethereal existence. It seemed to me that we alone had succeeded in thus conveying money, directly and without mediation, from one world to another. Others, indeed, had done so by the interposition of a medium, or by subscription to an occult magazine, but we had performed the feat with such simplicity that I was anxious to make our experience public, for the benefit of others like myself.

Annerly, however, was averse from this course, being fearful that it might break off our relations with Q.

It was some three months after our first inter-astral psycho-monetary experiment, that there came the culmination of my experiences—so mysterious as to leave me still lost in perplexity.

Annerly had come in to see me one afternoon. He looked nervous and depressed.

'I have just had a psychic communication from Q,' he said in answer to my inquiries, 'which I can hardly fathom. As far as I can judge, Q has formed some plan for interesting other phantasms in the kind of work that we are doing. He proposes to form, on his side of the gulf, an association that is to work in harmony with us, for monetary dealings on a large scale, between the two worlds.'

My reader may well imagine that my eyes almost

blazed with excitement at the magnitude of the prospect opened up.

'Q wishes us to gather together all the capital that we can, and to send it across to him, in order that he may be able to organise with him a corporate association of phanograms, or perhaps in this case, one would more correctly call them phantoids.'

I had no sooner grasped Annerly's meaning than I became enthusiastic over it.

We decided to try the great experiment that night.

My own worldly capital was, unfortunately, no great amount. I had, however, some £500 in bank stock left to me at my father's decease, which I could, of course, realise within a few hours. I was fearful, however, lest it might prove too small to enable Q to organise his fellow phantoids with it.

I carried the money in notes and sovereigns to Annerly's room, where it was laid on the table. Annerly was fortunately able to contribute a larger sum, which, however, he was not to place beside mine until after I had withdrawn, in order that conjunction of our monetary personalities might not dematerialise the astral phenomenon.

We made our preparations this time with exceptional care, Annerly quietly confident, I, it must be confessed, extremely nervous and fearful of failure. We removed our boots, and walked about on our stockinged feet, and at Annerly's suggestion, not only placed the furniture as before, but turned the coal-scuttle upside down, and laid a wet towel over the top of the wastepaper basket.

All complete, I wrung Annerly's hand, and went out into the darkness.

I waited next morning in vain. Nine o'clock came, ten

o'clock, and finally eleven, and still no word of him. Then feverish with anxiety, I sought his lodgings.

Judge of my utter consternation to find that Annerly had disappeared. He had vanished as if off the face of the earth. By what awful error in our preparations, by what neglect of some necessary psychic precautions, he had met his fate, I cannot tell. But the evidence was only too clear, that Annerly had been engulfed into the astral world, carrying with him the money for the transfer of which he had risked his mundane existence.

The proof of his disappearance was easy to find. As soon as I dared do so with discretion I ventured upon a few inquiries. The fact that he had been engulfed while still owing four months' rent for his rooms, and that he had vanished without even having time to pay such bills as he had outstanding with local tradesmen, showed that he must have been devisualised at a moment's notice.

The awful fear that I might be held accountable for his death, prevented me from making the affair public.

Till that moment I had not realised the risks that he had incurred in our reckless dealing with the world of spirits. Annerly fell a victim to the great cause of psychic science, and the record of our experiments remains in the face of prejudice as a witness to its truth.

FROM *Nonsense Novels*

Motion Study Tonsils

by Frank B. Gilbreth
and Ernestine Gilbreth Carey

Dad thought the best way to deal with sickness in the family was simply to ignore it.

'We don't have time for such nonsense,' he said. 'There are too many of us. A sick person drags down the performance of the entire group. You children come from sound pioneer stock. You've been given health, and it's your job to keep it. I don't want any excuses. I want you to stay well.'

Except for measles and whooping cough, we obeyed orders. Doctors' visits were so infrequent we learned to identify them with Mother's having a baby.

Dad's mother, who lived with us for a while, had her own secret for warding off disease. Grandma Gilbreth was born in Maine, where she said the seasons were Winter, July and August. She claimed to be an expert in combating cold weather and in avoiding head colds.

Her secret prophylaxis was a white bag, filled and saturated with camphor, which she kept hidden in her bosom. Grandma's bosom offered ample hiding space not only for camphor but for her eyeglasses, her handkerchief, and, if need be, for the bedspread she was crocheting.

Each year, as soon as the first frost appeared, she made twelve, identical white, camphor-filled bags for each of us.

'Mind what Grandma says and wear these all the time,' she told us. 'Now if you bring home a cold it will be your own blessed fault, and I'll skin you alive.'

Grandma always was threatening to skin someone alive, or draw and quarter him, or scalp him like a Red Indian, or spank him till his bottom blistered.

Grandma averred she was a great believer in 'spare the rod and spoil the child'. Her own personal rod was a branch from the lilac bush, which grew in the side lawn. She always kept a twig from this bush on the top of her dresser.

'I declare, you're going to catch it now,' she would say. 'Your mother won't spank you and your father is too busy to spank you, but your grandma is going to spank you till your bottom blisters.'

Then she would swing the twig with a vigour which belied her years. Most of her swings were aimed so as merely to whistle harmlessly through the air. She'd land a few light licks on our legs, though, and since we didn't want to hurt her feelings we'd scream and holler as if we were receiving the twenty-one lashes from a Spanish inquisitor. Sometimes she'd switch so vigorously at nothing that the twig would break.

'Ah, you see? You were so bad that I had to break my whip on you. Now go right out in the yard and cut me another one for next time. A big, thick one that will hurt even more than this one. Go along now. March!'

On the infrequent occasions when one of us did become sick enough to stay in bed, Grandma and Dad thought the best treatment was the absent treatment.

'A child abed mends best if left to himself,' Grandma said, while Dad nodded approval. Mother said she

61

agreed, too, but then she proceeded to wait on the sick child hand and foot.

'Here, darling, put my lovely bed jacket around your shoulders,' Mother would tell the ailing one. 'Here are some magazines, and scissors and paste. Now how's that? I'm going down to the kitchen and fix you a tray. Then I'll be up and read to you.'

A cousin brought measles into the house, and all of us except Martha, were stricken simultaneously. Two big adjoining bedrooms upstairs were converted into hospital wards—one for the boys and the other for the girls. We suffered together for two or three miserable, feverish, itchy days, while Mother applied cocoa butter and ice packs. Dr Burton, who had delivered most of us, said there was nothing to worry about. He was an outspoken man, and he and Dad understood each other.

'I'll admit, Gilbreth, that your children don't get sick very often,' Dr Burton said, 'but when they do it messes up the public health statistics for the entire state of New Jersey.'

'How come, Mr Bones?' Dad asked.

'I have to turn in a report every week on the number of contagious diseases I handle. Ordinarily, I handle a couple of cases of measles a week. When I report that I had eleven cases in a single day, they're liable to quarantine the whole town of Montclair and close up every school in Essex County.'

'Well, they're probably exceptionally light cases,' Dad said. 'Pioneer stock, you know.'

'As far as I'm concerned, measles is measles, and they've got the measles.'

'Probably even pioneers got the measles,' Dad said.

'Probably so. Pioneers had tonsils, too, and so do your kids. Really ugly tonsils. They ought to come out.'

'I never had mine out.'

'Let me see them,' Dr Burton ordered.

'There's nothing the matter with them.'

'For God's sake don't waste my time,' said Dr Burton. 'Open your mouth and say "Ah".'

Dad opened his mouth and said 'Ah.'

'I thought so,' Dr Burton nodded. 'Yours ought to come out too. Should have had them taken out years ago. I don't expect you to admit it, but you have sore throats, don't you? You have one right this, minute, haven't you?'

'Nonsense,' said Dad. 'Never sick a day in my life.'

'Well, let yours stay in if you want. You're not hurting anybody but yourself. But you really should have the children's taken out.'

'I'll talk it over with Lillie,' Dad promised.

Once the fever from the measles had gone, we all felt fine, although we still had to stay in bed. We sang songs, told continued stories, played spelling games and riddles, and had pillow-fights. Dad spent considerable time with us, joining in the songs and all the games except pillow-fights, which were illegal. He still believed in letting sick children alone, but, with all of us sick—or all but Martha, at any rate—he became so lonesome he couldn't stay away.

He came to the wards one night after supper, and took a chair over in a corner. We noticed that his face was covered with spots.

'Daddy,' asked Anne, 'what's the matter with you? You're all broken out in spots.'

'You're imagining things,' said Dad, smirking. 'I'm all right.'

'You've got the measles.'

'I'm all right,' said Dad. 'I can take it.'

'Daddy's got the measles, Daddy's got the measles.'

Dad sat there grinning, but our shouts were enough to bring Grandma on the run.

'What's the matter here?' she asked. And then to Dad, 'Mercy sakes, Frank, you're covered with spots.'

'It's just a joke,' Dad told his mother, weakly.

'Get yourself to bed. A man your age ought to know better. Shame on you.'

Grandma fumbled down her dress and put on her glasses. She peered into Dad's face.

'I declare, Frank Gilbreth,' she told him, 'sometimes I think you're more trouble than all of your children. Red ink! And you think it's a joke to scare a body half to death. Red ink!'

'A joke,' Dad repeated.

'Very funny,' Grandma muttered as she stalked out of the room. 'I'm splitting my sides.'

Dad sat there glumly.

'Is it red ink, Daddy?' we asked, and we agreed with him that it was, indeed, a very good joke. 'Is it? You really had us fooled.'

'You'll have to ask your grandma,' Dad sulked. 'She's a very smart lady. She knows it all.'

Martha, who appeared immune to measles, nevertheless wasn't allowed to come into the wards. She couldn't go to school, since the house was quarantined, and the week or two of being an 'only child' made her so miserable that she lost her appetite. Finally, she couldn't stand it any more, and sneaked into the sick rooms to visit us.

'You know you're not allowed in here,' said Anne. 'Do you want to get sick?'

Martha burst into tears. 'Yes,' she sobbed. 'Oh, yes.'

'Don't tell us you miss us? Why, I should think it would be wonderful to have the whole downstairs to

yourself, and be able to have Mother and Dad all by
yourself at dinner.'

'Dad's no fun any more,' said Mart. 'He's nervous. He
says the quiet at the table is driving him crazy.'

'Tell him that's not of general interest,' said Ern.

It was shortly after the measles epidemic that Dad
started applying motion study to surgery to try to reduce
the time required for certain operations.

'Surgeons really aren't much different from skilled
mechanics,' Dad said, 'except that they're not so skilled.
If I can get to study their motions, I can speed them up.
The speed of an operation often means the difference
between life and death.'

At first, the surgeons he approached weren't very co-
operative.

'I don't think it will work,' one doctor told him. 'We
aren't dealing with machines. We're dealing with human
beings. No two human beings are alike, so no set of
motions could be used over and over again.'

'I know it will work,' Dad insisted. 'Just let me take
some moving pictures of operations and I'll show you.'

Finally he got permission to set up his movie equipment in an operating-room. After the film was developed
he put it in the projector which he kept in the parlour
and showed us what he had done.

In the background was a cross-section screen and a big
clock with 'GILBRETH' written across its face and a
hand which made a full revolution every second. Each
doctor and nurse was dressed in white, and had a number on his cap to identify him. The patient was on an
operating table in the foreground. Off to the left, clad in
a white sheet, was something that resembled a snow-
covered Alp. When the Alp turned around, it had a

stop-watch in its hand. And when it smiled at the camera you could tell through the disguise that it was Dad.

It seemed to us, watching the moving pictures, that the doctors did a rapid, business-like job of a complicated abdominal operation. But Dad, cranking the projector behind us, kept hollering that it was 'stupidity incorporated'.

'Look at that boob—the doctor with No. 3 on his cap. Watch what he's going to do now. Walk all the way around the operating table. Now see him reach way over there for that instrument? And then he decides he doesn't want that one after all. He wants this one. He should call the instrument's name, and that nurse—No. 6, she's his caddy—should hand it to him. That's what she's there for. And look at his left hand—dangling there at his side. Why doesn't he use it? He could work twice as fast.'

The result of the moving picture was that the surgeons involved managed to reduce their ether time by fifteen per cent. Dad was far from satisfied. He explained that he needed to take moving pictures of five or six operations, all of the same type, so that he could sort out the good motions from the wasted motions. The trouble was that most patients refused to be photographed, and hospitals were afraid of law-suits.

'Never mind, dear,' Mother told him. 'I'm sure the opportunity will come along eventually for you to get all the pictures that you want.'

Dad said that he didn't like to wait; that when he started a project, he hated to put it aside and pick it up again piecemeal whenever he found a patient, hospital, and doctor who didn't object to photographs. Then an idea hit him, and he snapped his fingers.

'I know,' he said. 'I've got it. Dr Burton has been after me to have the kids' tonsils out. He says they really have to come out. We'll rig up an operating-room in the laboratory here, and take pictures of Burton.'

'It seems sort of heartless to use the children as guinea-pigs,' Mother said doubtfully.

'It does for a fact. And I won't do it unless Burton says it's perfectly all right. If taking pictures is going to make him nervous or anything, we'll have the tonsils taken out without the motion study.'

'Somehow or other I can't imagine Dr Burton being nervous,' Mother said.

'Me either. I'm going to call him. And you know what? I feel a little guilty about this whole deal. So, as conscience balm, I'm going to let the old butcher take mine out, too.'

'I feel a little guilty about the whole deal, too,' said Mother. 'Only thank goodness I had mine taken out when I was a girl.'

Dr Burton agreed to do the job in front of a movie camera.

'I'll save you for the last, Old Pioneer,' he told Dad. 'The best for last. Since the first day I laid eyes on your great, big, beautiful tonsils, I knew I wouldn't be content until I got my hands on them.'

'Stop drooling and put away your scalpel, you old flatterer you,' said Dad. 'I intend to be the last. I'll have mine out after the kids get better.'

Dr Burton said he would start with Anne and go right down the ladder, through Ernestine, Frank, Bill and Lillian.

Martha alone of the older children didn't need to have her tonsils out, the doctor said, and the children younger than Lillian could wait a while.

The night before the mass operation, Martha was told she would sleep at the house of Dad's oldest sister, Aunt Anne.

67

'I don't want you underfoot,' Dad informed her. 'The children who are going to have their tonsils out won't be able to have any supper tonight or breakfast in the morning. I don't want you around to lord it over them.'

Martha hadn't forgotten how we neglected her when she finally came down with the measles. She lorded it over us plenty before she finally departed.

'Aunt Anne always has apple pie for breakfast,' she said, which we all knew to be perfectly true, except that sometimes it was blueberry instead of apple. 'She keeps a jar of doughnuts in the pantry and she likes children to eat them.' This, too, was unfortunately no more than the simple truth. 'Tomorrow morning, when you are awaiting the knife, I will be thinking of you. I shall try, if I am not too full, to dedicate a doughnut to each of you.'

She rubbed her stomach with a circular motion, and puffed out her cheeks horribly as if she were chewing on a whole doughnut. She opened an imaginary doughnut jar and helped herself to another, which she rammed into her mouth.

'My goodness, Aunt Anne,' she said, pretending that that lady was in the room, 'those doughnuts are even more delicious than usual.' . . . 'Well, why don't you have another, Martha?' . . . 'Thanks, Aunt Anne, I believe I will.' . . . 'Why don't you take two or three, Martha?' . . . 'I'm so full of apple pie I don't know whether I could eat two more, Aunt Anne. But since it makes you happy to have people eat your cooking, I will do my best.'

'Hope you choke, Martha, dear,' we told her.

The next morning, the five of us selected to give our tonsils for motion study assembled in the parlour. As Martha had predicted, our stomachs were empty. They growled and rumbled. We could hear beds being moved around upstairs, and we knew the wards were being set up again. In the laboratory, which adjoined the parlour, Dad, his movie camera-man, a nurse and Dr Burton were converting a desk into an operating table, and setting up the cross-section background and lights.

Dad came into the parlour, dressed like an Alp again. 'All right, Anne, come on.' He thumped her on the back and smiled at the rest of us. 'There's nothing to it. It will be over in just a few minutes. And think of the fun we'll have looking at the movies and seeing how each of you looks when he's asleep.'

As he and Anne went out, we could see that his hands were trembling. Sweat was beginning to pop through his white robe. Mother came in and sat with us. Dad had wanted her to watch the operations, but she said she couldn't. After a while we heard Dad and a nurse walking heavily up the front stairs, and we knew Anne's operation was over and she was being carried to bed.

'I know I'm next, and I won't say I'm not scared,' Ernestine confided. 'But I'm so hungry all I can think of is Martha and that pie. The lucky dog.'

'And doughnuts,' said Bill. 'The lucky dog.'

'Can we have pie and doughnuts after our operations?' Lill asked Mother.

'If you want them,' said Mother, who had had her tonsils out.

Dad came into the room. His robe was dripping sweat now. It looked as if the spring thaw had come to the Alps.

'Nothing to it,' he said. 'And I know we got some great movies. Anne slept just like a baby. All right, Ernestine, girl. You're next; let's go.'

'I'm not hungry any more,' she said. 'Now I'm just scared.'

A nurse put a napkin saturated with ether over Ern's nose. The last thing she remembered was Mr Coggin, Dad's photographer, grinding away at the camera. 'He should be cranking at two revolutions a second,' she thought. 'I'll count and see if he is. And one and two and three and four. That's the way Dad says to count seconds. You have to put the "and" in between the numbers to count at the right speed. And one and two and three . . .' She fell asleep.

Dr Burton peered into her mouth.

'My God, Gilbreth,' he said. 'I told you I didn't want Martha.'

'You haven't got Martha,' Dad said. 'That's Ernestine.'

'Are you sure?'

'Of course I'm sure, you jackass. Don't you think I know my own children?'

'You must be mistaken,' Dr Burton insisted. 'Look at her carefully. There, now, isn't that Martha?'

'You mean to say you think I can't tell one child from another?'

'I don't mean to say anything, except if that isn't Martha we've made a horrible mistake.'

'We?' Dad squealed. 'We? I've made no mistake. And I hope I'm wrong in imagining the sort of mistake you've made.'

'You see, all I know them by is their tonsils,' said Dr Burton. 'I thought these tonsils were Martha. They were the only pair that didn't have to come out.'

'No,' roared Dad. 'Oh, no!' Then growing indignant: 'Do you mean to tell me you knocked my little girl unconscious for no reason at all?'

'It looks as if I did just that, Gilbreth. I'm sorry but it's done. It was damned careless. But you do have an uncommon lot of them, and they all look just alike to me.'

'All right, Burton,' Dad said. 'Sorry I lost my temper. What do we do?'

'I'm going to take them out anyway. They'd have to come out eventually at any rate, and the worst part of an operation is dreading it beforehand. She's done her dreading, and there's no use to make her do it twice.'

As Dr Burton leaned over Ernestine, some reflex caused her to knee him in the mouth.

'Okay, Ernestine, if that's really your name,' he muttered. 'I guess I deserved that.'

As it turned out, Ernestine's tonsils were recessed and bigger than the doctor had expected. It was a little messy to get at them, and Mr Coggin, the movie camera-man, was sick in a waste-paper basket.

'Don't stop cranking,' Dad shouted at him, 'or your tonsils will be next. I'll pull them out by the roots myself. Crank, by jingo, crank.'

Mr Coggin cranked. When the operation was over, Dad and the nurse carried Ernestine upstairs.

When Dad came in the parlour to get Frank, he told Mother to send someone over to Aunt Anne's for Martha.

'Apple pie, doughnuts or not, she's going to have her tonsils out,' he said. 'I'm not going through another day like this one again in a hurry.'

Frank, Bill and Lillian had their tonsils out, in that order. Then Martha arrived, bawling, kicking and full of pie and doughnuts.

'You said I didn't have to have my tonsils out,' she screamed at the doctor. Before he could get her on the desk which served as the operating table, she kicked him in the stomach.

'The next time I come to your house,' he said to Dad

71

as soon as he could get his breath, 'I'm going to wear a chest protector and a catcher's mask.' Then to the nurse: 'Give some ether to Martha, if that's really her name.'

'Yes, I'm Martha,' she yelled through the towel. 'You're making a mistake.'

'I told you she was Martha,' Dad said triumphantly.

'I know,' Dr Burton said. 'Let's not go into that again. She's Martha, but I've named her tonsils Ernestine. Open your mouth, Martha, you sweet child, and let me get Ernestine's tonsils. Crank on, Mr Coggin. Your film may be the first photographic record of a man slowly going berserk.'

All of us felt terribly sick that afternoon, but Martha was in agony.

'It's a shame,' Grandma kept telling Martha, who was named for her and was her especial pet. 'They shouldn't have let you eat all that stuff and then brought you back here for the butchering. I don't care whether it was the doctor's fault or your father's fault. I'd like to skin them both alive and then scalp them like Red Indians.'

While we were recuperating, Dad spent considerable time with us, minimised our discomforts, and kept telling us we were just looking for sympathy.

'Don't tell me,' he said. 'I saw the operations, didn't I? Why, there's only the little, tiniest cut at the back of your throat. I don't understand how you can do all that complaining. Don't you remember the story about the Spartan boy who kept his mouth shut while the fox was chewing on his vitals?'

It was partly because of our complaining, and the desire to show us how the Spartan boy would have had his tonsils out, that Dad decided to have only a local anaesthetic for his operation. Mother, Grandma and Dr Burton all advised against it. But Dad wouldn't listen.

'Why does everyone want to make a mountain out of a molehill over such a minor operation?' he said. 'I want to keep an eye on Burton and see that he doesn't mess up the job.'

The first day that we children were well enough to get up, Dad and Mother set out in the car for Dr Burton's office. Mother had urged Dad to call a taxi. She didn't know how to drive, and she said Dad probably wouldn't feel like doing the driving on the way home. But Dad laughed at her qualms.

'We'll be back in about an hour,' Dad called to us as he tested his three horns to make sure he was prepared for any emergency. 'Wait lunch for us. I'm starving.'

'You've got to hand it to him,' Anne admitted as the Pierce Arrow bucked up Wayside Place. 'He's the bee's knees, all right. We were all scared to death before our operations. And look at him. He's looking forward to it.'

Two hours later, a taxicab stopped in front of the house, and the driver jumped out and opened the door for his passengers. Then Mother emerged, pale and red-eyed. She and the driver helped a crumpled mass of moaning blue serge to alight. Dad's hat was rumpled and on sideways. His face was grey and sagging. He wasn't crying, but his eyes were watering. He couldn't speak and he couldn't smile.

'He's sure got a load on all right, Mrs Gilbreth,' said the driver enviously. 'And still early afternoon, too. Didn't even know he touched the stuff, myself.'

We waited for the lightning to strike, but it didn't. The seriousness of Dad's condition may be adjudged by the fact that he contented himself with a withering look.

'Keep a civil tongue in your head,' said Mother in one of the sharpest speeches of her career. 'He's deathly ill.'

Mother and Grandma helped Dad up to his room. We could hear him moaning, all the way downstairs.

Mother told us all about it that night, while Dad was snoring under the effects of sleeping pills. Mother had waited in Dr Burton's ante-room while the tonsillectomy was being performed. Dad had felt wonderful while under the local anaesthetic. When the operation was half over, he had come out into the ante-room, grinning and waving one tonsil on a pair of forceps.

'One down and one to go, Lillie,' he had said. 'Completely painless. Just like rolling off a log.'

After what had seemed an interminable time, Dad had come out into the waiting-room again, and reached for his hat and coat. He was still grinning, only not so wide as before.

'That's that,' he said. 'Almost painless. All right, boss, let's go. I'm still hungry.'

Then, as Mother watched, his high spirits faded and he began to fall to pieces.

'I'm stabbed,' he moaned. 'I'm haemorrhaging. Burton, come here. Quick! What have you done to me?'

Dr Burton came out of his office. It must be said to his credit that he was sincerely sympathetic. Dr Burton had had his own tonsils out.

'You'll be all right, Old Pioneer,' he said. 'You just had to have it the hard way.'

Dad obviously couldn't drive, so Mother had called the taxi. A man from the garage towed Foolish Carriage home later that night.

'I tried to drive it home,' the garage man told Mother, 'but I just couldn't budge it. I got the engine running all right, but it just spit and bucked every time I put it in gear. Durndest thing I ever saw.'

'I don't think anyone but Mr Gilbreth understands it,' Mother said.

Dad spent two weeks in bed, and it was the first time any of us remembered his being sick. He couldn't smoke, eat or talk. But he could glare, and he glared at Bill for two full minutes when Bill asked him one afternoon if he had had his tonsils taken out like the Spartans used to have theirs removed.

Dad didn't get his voice back until the very day that he finally got out of bed. He was lying there, propped up on pillows, reading his office mail. There was a card from Mr Coggin, the photographer.

'Hate to tell you, Mr Gilbreth, but none of your moving pictures came out. I forgot to take off the inside lens-cap. I'm terribly sorry. Coggin. P.S. I quit.'

Dad threw off the covers and reached for his bath-robe. For the first time in two weeks, he spoke:

'I'll track him down to the ends of the earth,' he croaked. 'I'll take a blunt button-hook and pull his tonsils out by the by-jingoed roots, just like I promised him. He doesn't quit. He's fired.' FROM *Cheaper by the Dozen*

Tooking for a Lowel

by Patrick Campbell

Even now, after all I have been through, the thought of being unclothed in the presence of women has the power to make me half mad with anxiety. I drum my feet on the floor, perspire and whistle loudly to drive the memory away.

So far, I, undressed, have come rushing at women twice. One of these occasions was connected with a shaving-brush.

I was lying in the bath one morning, when I remembered that I had left my new shaving-brush in my overcoat pocket. The overcoat was hanging in the hall.

Everything else was ready and in position. Shaving-mirror and soap; new razor-blade; toothbrush and paste; hairbrush, comb and brilliantine tin; packet of ginger biscuits and a copy of *Forever Amber* on a chair beside the bath. When I wash I like to *wash*.

Everything was ready, then, except the new shaving-brush. I lay submerged for some time with just the nostrils and the whites of the eyes showing, trying to think of a substitute for a shaving-brush. Perhaps if the soap were rubbed on with the hand, and worked in? Or the toothbrush might be adapted to serve the purpose? The only difference between a toothbrush and a shaving-brush is that one is shorter and harder than the other, and the handle is fastened on in a different direction. But the toothbrush, properly employed, might be induced to work up a lather. I might even, by accident, invent a new kind of shaving-brush, with a long handle and a scrubbing motion . . .

All this time I knew I would have to get out of the bath, and fetch the shaving-brush out of my overcoat pocket.

I got out of the bath, in the end, at a quarter past eleven. At that time I had a hairy kind of dressing-gown that set my teeth on edge if I put it on next to my skin. I ran out of the bathroom, roughly knotting a shirt about my waist.

In this flat the bathroom, bedroom and sitting-room led off a passage. I ran lightly down the passage to the door, where my overcoat usually hangs. Then I remembered I had left the coat lying on a chair in the sitting-room. I ran more rapidly back along the passage, leaving footprints on the carpet. Already, I was becoming chilled and a little pimply. Passing the bathroom door I put on an extra burst of speed, and entered the sitting-room nearly all out.

It is difficult under such circumstances to make a precise estimate of the passage of time, but I think that a fifth of a second elapsed before I saw the charwoman standing by the window. She must have been dusting the bureau, but when she saw me she froze dead.

I, too, froze. Then I said 'Waah!' and tried to leap out backwards through the door.

The charwoman very nearly got there first. The thought must have flashed through her mind that she would be better off outside in the passage, convenient to the main staircase, and so with a kind of loping run she came across the room.

We arrived upon the mat inside the door simultaneously. The mat went from under us, and we came down.

I fell heavily on the feather duster which she was carrying, and the bamboo handle snapped. I thought my leg had gone.

We lay together on the mat for several moments, not shouting or anything, just trying to piece together in a blurry way exactly what had happened.

I came to my senses first. I was younger than she was, and probably more resilient.

I jumped up and made another break for the door. To my surprise I found it was shut, and not only shut but locked. I wrenched at the handle, conscious in the most alive way of my appearance from the back. The door was unyielding. I caught sight of a Spanish shawl draped across the top of the piano, and in a trice I was enveloped in it, an unexpectedly flamboyant figure.

Afterwards I remembered that the door opened *outwards*. I had gained the impression that it was locked by unthinkingly pulling it towards me.

And now the charwoman was also back on her feet. But to my horror I saw that she was taking off her housecoat—slowly and deliberately. It seemed to be her intention to disrobe. But why?

I watched her, wide-eyed. She folded the housecoat into a neat square. She placed it tidily in the centre of the table. 'That,' she said, 'is me notice—and now me husband will have to be tole.'

I fortunately never saw her again.

The other incident involving me and women took place when I was fourteen.

On this occasion I was again lying in the bath, but this time it was night, and I was reading *The Boy's Own Paper*. The rest of my family had gone out to the theatre, and I was alone in the house.

The particular edition of *The Boy's Own Paper* which I was reading must have contained a number of bumper tales, because when I came to the last page I found that the temperature of the bathwater had dropped from near-boiling to lukewarm. Checking back later I discovered that this had, in fact, been my longest sitting—ninety-seven minutes.

Taking care not to disturb the water, and set up cold currents, I reached out with one arm and dropped the *B.O.P.* over the side of the bath on to the floor. With the same hand I groped around in gingerly fashion for the towel.

There was no towel. I had placed it on the chair, but now it had gone. I sat up in the bath, chilled, and peered over the edge, hoping to find it on the floor. There was no towel. I sank back into the water again, trying, as it were, to *draw* it round me.

There was no towel in the bathroom of any kind. And slowly I was freezing to death. I stretched out my right leg and turned on the hot-water tap with my toe. Ice-cold water gushed out.

There was only one measure to be taken in this extreme emergency. I gathered my muscles, leaped out of the bath in a compact ball, wrapped the *B.O.P.* round me, wrenched open the bathroom door and fled down the short passage leading to the linen-cupboard. The linen-cupboard door was open. I shot into it, and slammed the door behind me. Absolutely instantaneously I discovered that our parlourmaid, a young girl named Alice, was in the linen-cupboard too.

What Alice and I did was to start screaming, steadily, into one another's faces. Alice, I think, believed that the Young Master had come for her at last.

In the end I got the door open again. It opened

inwards, so that I was compelled to advance upon Alice in order to get round the edge of it. Alice, still screaming, welcomed this move with an attempt to climb the linen-shelves and get out of the window.

I tried some word of explanation. What I said was: 'It's all right, Alice; I'm tooking for a lowel.' This had the effect of throwing her into a frenzy. She tried to put her head into a pillow-cover.

It was obvious that there was nothing more I could do, so I ran back into the bathroom, locked the door and listened at the keyhole until I heard her run down the passage to the hall, sobbing.

The only other thing I would like to say is that now, whenever I have a bath, I make a list of the things I am going to need, and check it carefully before entering the water.

FROM *Patrick Campbell's Omnibus*

The Gift of the Magi

by O. Henry

One dollar and eighty-seven cents. That was all. And sixty cents of it was in pennies. Pennies saved one and two at a time by bulldozing the grocer and the vegetable man and the butcher until one's cheeks burned with the silent imputation of parsimony that such close dealing implied. Three times Della counted it. One dollar and eighty-seven cents. And the next day would be Christmas.

There was clearly nothing to do but flop down on the shabby little couch and howl. So Della did it. Which instigates the moral reflection that life is made up of sobs, with sniffles predominating.

While the mistress of the home is gradually subsiding from the first stage to the second, take a look at the home. A furnished flat at $8 per week. It did not exactly beggar description, but it had certainly had that word on the lookout for the mendicancy squad.

In the vestibule below was a letter-box into which no letter would go, and an electric button from which no mortal finger could coax a ring. Also appertaining thereunto was a card bearing the name 'Mr James Dillingham Young.'

The 'Dillingham' had been flung to the breeze during a former period of prosperity when its possessor was being paid $30 per week. Now, when the income was shrunk to $20, the letters of 'Dillingham' looked blurred, as though they were thinking seriously of contracting to a modest and unassuming D. But whenever Mr James Dillingham Young came home and reached his flat above he was called 'Jim' and greatly hugged by Mrs James Dillingham Young, already introduced to you as Della. Which is all very good.

Della finished her cry and attended to her cheeks with the powder rag. She stood by the window and looked out dully at a gray cat walking a gray fence in a gray backyard. Tomorrow would be Christmas Day, and she had only $1.87 with which to buy Jim a present. She had been saving every penny she could for months, with this result. Twenty dollars a week doesn't go far. Expenses had been greater than she had calculated. They always are. Only $1.87 to buy a present for Jim. Her Jim. Many a happy hour she had spent planning for something nice for him. Something fine and rare and sterling—something just a little bit near to being worthy of the honour of being owned by Jim.

There was a pier-glass between the windows of the room. Perhaps you have seen a pier-glass in an $8 flat. A very thin and very agile person may, by observing his reflection in a rapid sequence of longitudinal strips, obtain a fairly accurate conception of his looks. Della, being slender, had mastered the art.

Suddenly she whirled from the window and stood before the glass. Her eyes were shining brilliantly, but her face had lost its colour within twenty seconds. Rapidly she pulled down her hair and let it fall to its length.

Now, there were two possessions of the James Dillingham Youngs in which they both took a mighty pride. One was Jim's gold watch that had been his father's and his grandfather's. The other was Della's hair. Had the

Queen of Sheba lived in the flat across the airshaft, Della would have let her hair hang out of the window some day to dry just to depreciate Her Majesty's jewels and gifts. Had King Solomon been the janitor, with all his treasure piled up in the basement, Jim would have pulled out his watch every time he passed, just to see him pluck at his beard from envy.

So now Della's beautiful hair fell about her rippling and shining like a cascade of brown waters. It reached below her knee and made itself almost a garment for her. And then she did it up again nervously and quickly. Once she faltered for a minute and stood still while a tear or two splashed on the worn red carpet.

On went her old brown jacket; on went her old brown hat. With a whirl of skirts and with the brilliant sparkle still in her eyes, she fluttered out the door and down the stairs to the street.

Where she stopped the sign read: 'Mme Sofronie. Hair Goods of All Kinds.' One flight up Della ran, and collected herself, panting. Madame, large, too white, chilly, hardly looked the 'Sofronie'.

'Will you buy my hair?' asked Della.

'I buy hair,' said Madame. 'Take yer hat off and let's have a sight at the looks of it.'

Down rippled the brown cascade.

'Twenty dollars,' said Madame, lifting the mass with a practised hand.

'Give it to me quick,' said Della.

Oh, and the next two hours tripped by on rosy wings. Forget the hashed metaphor. She was ransacking the stores for Jim's present.

She found it at last. It surely had been made for Jim and no one else. There was no other like it in any of the stores, and she had turned all of them inside out. It was a platinum fob chain simple and chaste in design, properly proclaiming its value by substance alone and not by meretricious ornamentation—as all good things should do. It was even worthy of The Watch. As soon as she saw it she knew that it must be Jim's. It was like him. Quietness and value—the description applied to both. Twenty-one dollars they took from her for it, and she hurried home with the 87 cents. With that chain on his watch Jim might be properly anxious about the time in any company. Grand as the watch was, he sometimes looked at it on the sly on account of the old leather strap that he used in place of a chain.

When Della reached home her intoxication gave way a little to prudence and reason. She got out her curling irons and lighted the gas and went to work repairing the ravages made by generosity added to love. Which is always a tremendous task, dear friends—a mammoth task.

Within forty minutes her head was covered with tiny, close-lying curls that made her look wonderfully like a truant schoolboy. She looked at her reflection in the mirror long, carefully and critically.

'If Jim doesn't kill me,' she said to herself, 'before he takes a second look at me, he'll say I look like a Coney Island chorus girl. But what could I do—oh! what could I do with a dollar and eighty-seven cents?'

At 7 o'clock the coffee was made and the frying-pan was on the back of the stove hot and ready to cook the chops.

Jim was never late. Della doubled the fob chain in her hand and sat on the corner of the table near the door that he always entered. Then she heard his step on the stair away on the first flight, and she turned white for just a moment. She had a habit of saying silent prayers

about the simplest everyday things, and now she whispered: 'Please God, make him think I am still pretty.'

The door opened and Jim stepped in and closed it.
He looked thin and very serious. Poor fellow, he was only
twenty-two—and to be burdened with a family! He
needed a new overcoat and he was without gloves.

Jim stopped inside the door, as immovable as a setter
at the scent of quail. His eyes were fixed upon Della, and
there was an expression in them that she could not read,
and it terrified her. It was not anger, nor surprise, nor
disapproval, nor horror, nor any of the sentiments that
she had been prepared for. He simply stared at her fixedly
with that peculiar expression on his face.

Della wriggled off the table and went to him.

'Jim, darling,' she cried, 'don't look at me that way.
I had my hair cut off and sold it because I couldn't have
lived through Christmas without giving you a present.
It'll grow out again—you won't mind, will you? I just
had to do it. My hair grows awfully fast. Say "Merry
Christmas!", Jim, and let's be happy. You don't know
what a nice—what a beautiful, nice gift I've got for
you.'

'You've cut off your hair?' asked Jim, laboriously, as
if he had not arrived at that patent fact yet even after
the hardest mental labour.

'Cut it off and sold it,' said Della. 'Don't you like me
just as well, anyhow? I'm me without my hair, ain't I?'

Jim looked about the room curiously.

'You say your hair is gone?' he said, with an air almost
of idiocy.

'You needn't look for it,' said Della. 'It's sold, I tell
you—sold and gone, too. It's Christmas Eve, boy. Be
good to me, for it went for you. Maybe the hairs of my
head were numbered,' she went on with a sudden serious

sweetness, 'but nobody could ever count my love for you. Shall I put the chops on, Jim?'

Out of his trance Jim seemed quickly to wake. He enfolded his Della. For ten seconds let us regard with discreet scrutiny some inconsequential object in the other direction. Eight dollars a week or a million a year— what is the difference? A mathematician or a wit would give you the wrong answer. The magi brought valuable gifts, but that was not among them. This dark assertion will be illuminated later on.

Jim drew a package from his overcoat pocket and threw it upon the table.

'Don't make any mistake, Dell,' he said, 'about me. I don't think there's anything in the way of a haircut or a shave or a shampoo that could make me like my girl any less. But if you'll unwrap that package you may see why you had me going a while at first.'

White fingers and nimble tore at the string and paper. And then an ecstatic scream of joy; and then, alas! a quick feminine change to hysterical tears and wails, necessitating the immediate employment of all the comforting powers of the lord of the flat.

For there lay The Combs—the set of combs, side and back, that Della had worshipped for long in a Broadway window. Beautiful combs, pure tortoise shell, with jewelled rims—just the shade to wear in the beautiful vanished hair. They were expensive combs, she knew, and her heart had simply craved and yearned over them without the least hope of possession. And now, they were hers, but the tresses that should have adorned the coveted adornments were gone.

But she hugged them to her bosom, and at length she was able to look up with dim eyes and a smile and say: 'My hair grows so fast, Jim!'

And then Della leaped up like a little singed cat and cried, 'Oh, oh!'

Jim had not yet seen his beautiful present. She held it out to him eagerly upon her open palm. The dull precious metal seemed to flash with a reflection of her bright and ardent spirit.

'Isn't it a dandy, Jim? I hunted all over the town to find it. You'll have to look at the time a hundred times a day now. Give me your watch. I want to see how it looks on it.'

Instead of obeying, Jim tumbled down on the couch and put his hands under the back of his head and smiled.

'Dell,' said he, 'let's put our Christmas presents away and keep 'em a while. They're too nice to use at present. I sold the watch to get the money to buy your combs. And now suppose you put the chops on.'

The magi, as you know, were wise men—wonderfully wise men—who brought gifts to the Babe in the manger. They invented the art of giving Christmas presents. Being wise, their gifts were no doubt wise ones, possibly bearing the privilege of exchange in case of duplication. And here I have lamely related to you the uneventful chronicle of two foolish children in a flat who most unwisely sacrificed for each other the greatest treasures of their house. But in a last word to the wise of these days let it be said that of all who give gifts these two were the wisest. Of all who give and receive gifts, such as they are wisest. Everywhere they are the wisest. They are the magi.

FROM *The Four Million*

The Sportsmen of Scowle

by Bernard Hollowood

The mining villages are traditionally the nurseries of our greatest performers in the world of Association Football. Scowle as I knew it some forty years ago was no exception. Yet Scowle's football was unique in many ways. For one thing the playing season was of an indeterminate length, varying according to the success of the team. If the opening matches were lost and the team had no chance of figuring in the struggle for the championship of the Mercian League a sudden halt would be called in the programme, all remaining fixtures would be scratched and Saturday afternoons would be given up to whippet-racing or ratting.

This practice earned Scowle an unenviable sporting reputation and on the few occasions their womenfolk permitted them to play away from home the team had a very hostile reception.

It is often said jokingly of the Scots that they can recruit a new centre-forward merely by shouting for one down the shaft of any Lanarkshire colliery. That story is almost literally true of Scowle. More than once, as a boy, I have seen my father, the trainer-manager of the club, race to the pit-head just before the kick-off and scrawl a message on a descending coal-tub:

'Left-back, centre-half, two inside-forwards and a linesman, immediately. *Floreat* Scowle!'—and inside five minutes the gaps in the eleven would be filled. The only position in the team that could not be filled in this way was the goalkeeper's. A player's risk as a moving target was serious enough; it was practically suicide to gamble with the demonstrative ire of a spectator of Scowle by standing relatively immobile between the goalposts.

In 1901 Scowle A.F.C. enjoyed one of its most successful seasons. A fixture-list of twenty-eight matches was completed without a single defeat, and the team won the championship and the League cup. In a way there was an element of luck about both achievements, for several of the strongest teams had to forfeit points for failing to appear at the Scowle ground. Cannock Rovers were particularly unfortunate, perhaps, for their loaded brake disappeared down a disused pit-shaft and was never recovered. My grandfather Ebby was greatly upset by the news of the disaster, for it was his route across the fells that the Cannock driver had been following.

I will now tell what I know of the famous and oft-discussed semi-final of the same season. Like all women in Scowle, my mother detested football and she did everything in her power to prevent my brother Caleb from playing in the match. On the Friday night it became obvious that she had seized and secreted his football boots, and the combined pleading of my father, Caleb and myself failed to soften her attitude.

In the still hours of Saturday morning, while my mother was still asleep, my father and my brother Caleb arose and by candlelight and in stockinged feet began to hunt for the missing boots. They had just completed their search of the parlour when my father stubbed his toe against one of old Ebby's gadgets for preventing draughts. He stifled a groan and listened. Upstairs, my mother was already moving. My father and Caleb blew out their candles and crouched behind the harmonium.

My mother came downstairs in her clogs and night-dress. She collected the poker from the kitchen and ran into the parlour. Then holding her taper aloft she tiptoed to the old oak chest, lifted the lid, gasped at the disorder of the heirlooms within, ran to the front door and yelled for help.

' 'Elp, 'elp, 'elp!' she screamed. 'We'n bin robbed!' My father and my brother Caleb darted upstairs, held a brief consultation and darted down again.

The street was now fully awake and men were running to and fro swinging their pit-lamps and cursing. From the window of my room I saw my father rush out into the night. I saw lights converge and form a circle about him. For a few moments there was silence. Then the group broke up and the men ran bellowing to our cottage. They swarmed in through the front door and soon filled every room with uproar and commotion. And as they searched for the burglar they shouted to my mother who made frantic efforts to restrain them.

'Dinna tha fret, missus,' they said. 'We'n find th'divil if 'e be rightly 'ere.'

In their excitement they looked into the oddest places —into drawers and boxes, under piles of linen, into saucepans and earthenware receptacles. And, at last, when they had made every room a shambles, the five o'clock hooter sounded and they trooped off to work at Orange No. 2 Pit.

My brother Caleb played against Dudley Wanderers that afternoon; and he played in his own boots, which were handed to him by Jem Clemlow shortly before the kick-off. The strangest thing about this episode was that my mother never referred to the boots and Jem Clemlow would not divulge where he had found them or what they were wrapped in.

Saul Crabb and Ephraim Tellwright were less fortunate than my brother Caleb. During the morning shift a light explosion occurred in the Dribben seam and several tons of roof caved in, cutting off five men, including the left-half and outside-right. A rescue party soon made contact with the trapped men and offered to start digging them out there and then. But Saul Crabb and Ephraim Tellwright signalled that the match must go on, that they had enough oxygen to last for at least eight hours. Two comparatively raw recruits were drafted into the eleven to fill the vacancies.

We now come to the match itself. Dudley won the toss and kicked with the wind, grit and smoke from the 'Disaster' end. They were a very fast team and inside ten minutes had obtained a lead of three goals. The spectators bided their time with complete confidence in Scowle's recuperative powers.

At half-time Dudley led by seven goals to nil and the referee, a man of considerable experience, was taken ill. Mr Chalmers, the village constable, agreed to deputise for him.

The game continued to go badly for Scowle after the interval and with only twenty-five minutes left for play it became obvious that Dudley's losses—they now had only seven effective men—were not going to prove serious enough. I was standing near my father and Dr Warburton at this critical moment. I saw them retreat from the touchline and stand with their backs to the game in earnest conversation. I saw the doctor open his bag. Then they returned to their former stations but almost immediately my father ran on to the field to assist a fallen Dudley player. I saw him press the man's head between his knees and dab at his face repeatedly with his sponge.

My father was on the field for practically the whole of the next five minutes and whether they were injured or not the Dudley players received persistent attention with his sponge.

After this Scowle ran their opponents off their legs. Dudley seemed helpless. Their remaining men staggered and lurched round the field like drunkards while Scowle scored goal after goal. And when the final whistle blew the home team were victors by three clear goals. My brother Caleb scored a double hat-trick.

The Dudley club lodged a number of protests, some of them, like the one relating to my father's sponge, being quite ridiculous. The League committee very properly dismissed them all.

As soon as the match was over Dr Warburton raced to the colliery with the rescue party. For hours on end he worked gallantly tending rescued and rescuers alike, and when one man wielded his pick carelessly he performed a delicate operation on the victim by the light of a single pit-lamp—and what was even more remarkable perhaps, without using chloroform.

FROM *Scowle and Other Papers*

The Strange Case of Mr Donnybrook's Boredom

by Ogden Nash

Once upon a time there was a man named Mr Donnybrook.
*

He was married to a woman named Mrs Donnybrook.
*

Mr and Mrs Donnybrook dearly loved to be bored.
*

Sometimes they were bored at the ballet, other times at
the cinema.
*

They were bored riding elephants in India and eleva-
tors in the Empire State Building.
*

They were bored in speakeasies during Prohibition and
in cocktail lounges after Repeal.
*

They were bored by Grand Dukes and garbagemen,
debutantes and demimondaines, opera singers and
operations.
*

They scoured the Five Continents and the Seven Seas in
their mad pursuit of boredom.
*

This went on for years and years.

*

One day Mr Donnybrook turned to Mrs Donnybrook.

*

My dear, he said, we have reached the end of our rope.

*

We have exhausted every yawn.

*

The world holds nothing more to jade our titillated palates.

*

Well, said Mrs Donnybrook, we might try insomnia.

*

So they tried insomnia.

*

About two o'clock the next morning Mr Donnybrook said, My, insomnia is certainly quite boring, isn't it?

*

Mrs Donnybrook said it certainly was, wasn't it?

*

Pretty soon he began to count sheep.

*

Mrs Donnybrook began to count sheep, too.

*

After awhile Mr Donnybrook said, Hey, you're counting my sheep!

*

Stop counting my sheep, said Mr Donnybrook.

*

Why, the very idea, said Mrs Donnybrook.

*

I guess I know my own sheep, don't I?

*

How? said Mr Donnybrook.

*

They're cattle, said Mrs Donnybrook.

*

They're cattle, and longhorns at that.

*

Furthermore, said Mrs Donnybrook, us cattle ranchers is shore tired o' you sheepmen plumb ruinin' our water.

*

I give yuh fair warnin', said Mrs Donnybrook, yuh better get them woolly Gila monsters o' yourn back across the Rio Grande afore mornin' or I'm a goin' to string yuh up on the nearest cottonwood.

*

Carramba! sneered Mr Donnybrook. Thees ees free range, no?

*

No, said Mrs Donnybrook, not for sheep men.

*

She strung him up on the nearest cottonwood.

*

Mr Donnybrook had never been so bored in his life.

FROM *Bed Riddance*

First Confession

by Frank O'Connor

All the trouble began when my grandfather died and my grandmother—my father's mother—came to live with us. Relations in the one house are a strain at the best of times, but, to make matters worse, my grandmother was a real old countrywoman and quite unsuited to the life in town. She had a fat, wrinkled old face, and, to Mother's great indignation, went round the house in bare feet—the boots had her crippled, she said. For dinner she had a jug of porter and a pot of potatoes with —sometimes—a bit of salt fish, and she poured out the potatoes on the table and ate them, slowly, with great relish, using her fingers by way of a fork.

Now, girls are supposed to be fastidious, but I was the one who suffered most from this. Nora, my sister, just sucked up to the old woman for the penny she got every Friday out of the old-age pension, a thing I could not do. I was too honest, that was my trouble; and when I was playing with Bill Connell, the sergeant major's son, and saw my grandmother steering up the path with a jug of porter sticking out from beneath her shawl I was mortified. I made excuses not to let him come into the house, because I could never be sure what she would be up to when we went in.

When Mother was at work and my grandmother made dinner I wouldn't touch it. Nora once tried to make me, but I hid under the table from her and took the bread-knife with me for protection. Nora let on to be very indignant (she wasn't, of course, but she knew Mother saw through her, so she sided with Gran) and came after me. I lashed out at her with the bread-knife, and after that she left me alone. I stayed there till Mother came in from work and made my dinner, but when Father came in later Nora said in a shocked voice: 'Oh, Dadda, do you know what Jackie did at dinnertime?' Then, of course, it all came out; Father gave me a flaking; Mother interfered, and for days after that he didn't speak to me and Mother barely spoke to Nora. And all because of that old woman! God knows, I was heart-scalded.

Then, to crown my misfortunes, I had to make my first confession and communion. It was an old woman called Ryan who prepared us for these. She was about the one age with Gran; she was well-to-do, lived in a big house on Montenotte, wore a black cloak and bonnet, and came every day to school at three o'clock when we should have been going home, and talked to us of hell. She may have mentioned the other place as well, but that could only have been by accident, for hell had the first place in her heart.

She lit a candle, took out a new half-crown and offered it to the first boy who would hold one finger—only one finger!—in the flame for five minutes by the school clock. Being always very ambitious I was tempted to volunteer, but I thought it might look greedy. Then she asked were we afraid of holding one finger—only one finger!—in a little candle flame for five minutes and not afraid of burning all over in roasting hot furnaces for all eternity. 'All eternity! Just think of that! A whole lifetime goes by and it's nothing, not even a drop in the ocean of your sufferings.' The woman was really interesting about hell, but my attention was all fixed on the half-crown. At the end of the lesson she put it back in her purse. It was a great disappointment; a religious woman like that, you wouldn't think she'd bother about a thing like a half-crown.

Another day she said she knew a priest who woke one night to find a fellow he didn't recognise leaning over the end of his bed. The priest was a bit frightened—naturally enough—but he asked the fellow what he wanted, and the fellow said in a deep, husky voice that he wanted to go to confession. The priest said it was an awkward time and wouldn't it do in the morning, but the fellow said that the last time he went to confession, there was one sin he kept back, being ashamed to mention it, and now it was always on his mind. Then the priest knew it was a bad case, because the fellow was after making a bad confession and committing a mortal sin. He got up to dress, and just then the cock crew in the yard outside, and—lo and behold!—when the priest looked round there was no sign of the fellow, only a smell of burning timber, and when the priest looked at his bed didn't he see the print of two hands burned in it? That was because the fellow had made a bad confession. This story made a shocking impression on me.

But the worst of all was when she showed us how to examine our conscience. Did we take the name of the Lord, our God, in vain? Did we honour our father and our mother? (I asked her did this include grandmothers and she said it did.) Did we love our neighbours as ourselves? Did we covet our neighbour's goods? (I thought of the way I felt about the penny that Nora got every Friday.) I decided that, between one thing and another, I must have broken the whole ten commandments, all on account of that old woman, and so far as I could see, so long as she remained in the house I had no hope of ever doing anything else.

I was scared to death of confession. The day the whole class went I let on to have a toothache, hoping my absence wouldn't be noticed; but at three o'clock, just as I was feeling safe, along comes a chap with a message from Mrs Ryan that I was to go to confession myself on Saturday and be at the chapel for communion with the rest. To make it worse, Mother couldn't come with me and sent Nora instead.

Now, that girl had ways of tormenting me that Mother never knew of. She held my hand as we went down the hill, smiling sadly and saying how sorry she was for me, as if she were bringing me to the hospital for an operation.

'Oh, God help us!' she moaned. 'Isn't it a terrible pity you weren't a good boy? Oh, Jackie, my heart bleeds for you! How will you ever think of all your sins? Don't forget you have to tell him about the time you kicked Gran on the shin.'

'Lemme go!' I said, trying to drag myself free of her. 'I don't want to go to confession at all.'

'But sure, you'll have to go to confession, Jackie,' she replied in the same regretful tone. 'Sure, if you didn't, the parish priest would be up to the house looking for you. 'Tisn't, God knows, that I'm not sorry for you. Do you remember the time you tried to kill me with the bread-knife under the table? And the language you used to me? I don't know what he'll do with you at all, Jackie. He might have to send you up to the bishop.'

I remember thinking bitterly that she didn't know the half of what I had to tell—if I told it. I knew I couldn't tell it, and understood perfectly why the fellow in Mrs Ryan's story made a bad confession; it seemed to me a great shame that people wouldn't stop criticising him. I

remember that steep hill down to the church, and the
sunlit hillsides beyond the valley of the river, which I
saw in the gaps between the houses like Adam's last
glimpse of Paradise.

Then, when she had manœuvred me down the long
flight of steps to the chapel yard, Nora suddenly changed
her tone. She became the malicious devil she really was.

'There you are!' she said with a yelp of triumph, hurl-
ing me through the church door. 'And I hope he'll give
you the penitential psalms, you dirty little caffler.'

I knew then I was lost, given up to eternal justice. The
door with the coloured-glass panels swung shut behind
me, the sunlight went out and gave place to deep shadow,
and the wind whistled outside so that the silence within
seemed to crackle like ice under my feet. Nora sat in
front of me by the confession box. There were a couple
of old women ahead of her, and then a miserable-looking
poor devil came and wedged me in at the other side, so
that I couldn't escape even if I had the courage. He
joined his hands and rolled his eyes in the direction of
the roof, muttering aspirations in an anguished tone,
and I wondered had he a grandmother too. Only a
grandmother could account for a fellow behaving in that
heartbroken way, but he was better off than I, for he at
least could go and confess his sins; while I would make a
bad confession and then die in the night and be continually coming back and burning people's furniture.

Nora's turn came, and I heard the sound of something
slamming, and then her voice as if butter wouldn't melt
in her mouth, and then another slam, and out she came.
God, the hypocrisy of women! Her eyes were lowered,
her head was bowed, and her hands were joined very
low down on her stomach, and she walked up the aisle
to the side altar looking like a saint. You never saw such

an exhibition of devotion; and I remembered the devilish malice with which she had tormented me all the way from our door, and wondered were all religious people like that, really. It was my turn now. With the fear of damnation in my soul I went in, and the confessional door closed of itself behind me.

It was pitch-dark and I couldn't see priest or anything else. Then I really began to be frightened. In the darkness it was a matter between God and me, and He had all the odds. He knew what my intentions were before I even started; I had no chance. All I had ever been told about confession got mixed up in my mind and I knelt to one wall and said: 'Bless me, father, for I have sinned; this is my first confession.' I waited for a few minutes, but nothing happened, so I tried it on the other wall. Nothing happened there either. He had me spotted all right.

It must have been then that I noticed the shelf at about one height with my head. It was really a place for grown-up people to rest their elbows, but in my distracted state I thought it was probably the place you were supposed to kneel. Of course, it was on the high side and not very deep, but I was always good at climbing and managed to get up all right. Staying up was the trouble. There was room only for my knees, and nothing you could get a grip on but a sort of wooden moulding a bit above it. I held on to the moulding and repeated the words a little louder and this time something happened all right. A slide was slammed back; a little light entered the box, and a man's voice said: 'Who's there?'

' 'Tis me, father,' I said for fear he mightn't see me and go away again. I couldn't see him at all. The place the voice came from was under the moulding, about level with my knees, so I took a good grip of the moulding and swung myself down till I saw the astonished face of a young priest looking up at me. He had to put his head on one side to see me, and I had to put mine on one side to see him, so we were more or less talking to one another upside-down. It struck me as a queer way of hearing confessions, but I didn't feel it my place to criticise.

'Bless me, father, for I have sinned; this is my first confession,' I rattled off all in one breath, and swung myself down the least shade more to make it easier for him.

'What are you doing up there?' he shouted in an angry voice, and the strain the politeness was putting on my hold of the moulding, and the shock of being addressed in such an uncivil tone, were too much for me. I lost my grip, tumbled and hit the door an unmerciful wallop before I found myself flat on my back in the middle of the aisle. The people who had been waiting stood up with their mouths open. The priest opened the door of the middle box and came out, pushing his biretta back from his forehead; he looked something terrible. Then Nora came scampering down the aisle.

'Oh, you dirty little caffler!' she said. 'I might have known you'd do it. I might have known you'd disgrace me. I can't leave you out of my sight for one minute.'

Before I could even get to my feet to defend myself she bent down and gave me a clip across the ear. This reminded me that I was so stunned I had even forgotten to cry, so that people might think I wasn't hurt at all, when in fact I was probably maimed for life. I gave a roar out of me.

'What's all this about?' the priest hissed, getting angrier than ever and pushing Nora off me. 'How dare you hit the child like that, you little vixen?'

'But I can't do my penance with him, father,' Nora cried, cocking an outraged eye up at him.

'Well, go and do it, or I'll give you some more to do,' he said, giving me a hand up. 'Was it coming to confession you were, my poor man?' he asked me.

' 'Twas, father,' said I with a sob.

'Oh,' he said respectfully, 'a big hefty fellow like you must have terrible sins. Is this your first?'

' 'Tis, father,' said I.

'Worse and worse,' he said gloomily. 'The crimes of a lifetime. I don't know will I get rid of you at all today. You'd better wait now till I'm finished with these old ones. You can see by the looks of them they haven't much to tell.'

'I will, father,' I said with something approaching joy.

The relief of it was really enormous. Nora stuck out her tongue at me from behind his back, but I couldn't even be bothered retorting. I knew from the very moment that man opened his mouth that he was intelligent above the ordinary. When I had time to think, I saw how right I was. It stood to reason that a fellow confessing after seven years would have more to tell than people that went every week. The crimes of a lifetime, exactly as he said. It was only what he expected, and the rest was the cackle of old women and girls with their talk of hell, the bishop and the penitential psalms. That was all they knew. I started to make my examination of conscience, and barring the one bad business of my grandmother it didn't seem so bad.

The next time, the priest steered me into the confession box himself and left the shutter back the way I could see him get in and sit down at the further side of the grill from me.

'Well, now,' he said, 'what do they call you?'

'Jackie, father,' said I.

'And what's a-trouble to you, Jackie?'

'Father,' I said, feeling I might as well get it over while
I had him in good humour, 'I had it all arranged to kill
my grandmother.'

He seemed a bit shaken by that, all right, because he
said nothing for quite a while.

'My goodness,' he said at last, 'that'd be a shocking
thing to do. What put that into your head?'

'Father,' I said, feeling very sorry for myself, 'she's an
awful woman.'

'Is she?' he asked. 'What way is she awful?'

'She takes porter, father,' I said, knowing well from
the way Mother talked of it that this was a mortal sin,
and hoping it would make the priest take a more favour-
able view of my case.

'Oh, my!' he said, and I could see he was impressed.

'And snuff, father,' said I.

'That's a bad case, sure enough, Jackie,' he said.

'And she goes round in her bare feet, father,' I went
on in a rush of self pity, 'and she know I don't like her,
and she gives pennies to Nora and none to me, and my
da sides with her and flakes me, and one night I was so
heart-scalded I made up my mind I'd have to kill her.'

'And what would you do with the body?' he asked
with great interest.

'I was thinking I could chop that up and carry it away
in a barrow I have,' I said.

'Begor, Jackie,' he said, 'do you know you're a terrible
child?'

'I know, father,' I said, for I was just thinking the same
thing myself. 'I tried to kill Nora too with a bread-knife
under the table, only I missed her.'

'Is that the little girl that was beating you just now?'
he asked.

' 'Tis, father.'

'Someone will go for her with a bread-knife one day, and he won't miss her,' he said rather cryptically. 'You must have great courage. Between ourselves, there's a lot of people I'd like to do the same to but I'd never have the nerve. Hanging is an awful death.'

'Is it, father?' I asked with the deepest interest—I was always very keen on hanging. 'Did you ever see a fellow hanged?'

'Dozens of them,' he said solemnly. 'And they all died roaring.'

'Jay!' I said.

'Oh, a horrible death!' he said with great satisfaction. 'Lots of the fellows I saw killed their grandmothers too, but they all said 'twas never worth it.'

He had me there for a full ten minutes talking, and then he walked out the chapel yard with me. I was genuinely sorry to part with him, because he was the most entertaining character I'd ever met in the religious line. Outside, after the shadow of the church, the sunlight was like the roaring of waves on a beach; it dazzled me; and when the frozen silence melted and I heard the screech of trams on the road my heart soared. I knew now I wouldn't die in the night and come back, leaving marks on my mother's furniture. It would be a great worry to her, and the poor soul had enough.

Nora was sitting on the railing, waiting for me, and she put on a very sour puss when she saw the priest with me. She was mad jealous because a priest had never come out of the church with her.

'Well,' she asked coldly, after he left me, 'what did he give you?'

'Three Hail Marys,' I said.

'Three Hail Marys,' she repeated incredulously. 'You mustn't have told him anything.'

'I told him everything,' I said confidently.

'About Gran and all?'

'About Gran and all.'

(All she wanted was to be able to go home and say I'd made a bad confession.)

'Did you tell him you went for me with the bread-knife?' she asked with a frown.

'I did to be sure.'

'And he only gave you three Hail Marys?'

'That's all.'

She slowly got down from the railing with a baffled air. Clearly, this was beyond her. As we mounted the steps back to the main road she looked at me suspiciously.

'What are you sucking?' she asked.

'Bullseyes.'

'Was it the priest gave them to you?'

' 'Twas.'

'Lord God,' she wailed bitterly, 'some people have all the luck! 'Tis no advantage to anybody trying to be good. I might just as well be a sinner like you.'

FROM The Stories of Frank O'Connor

Safe and Soundproof

by Joan Aiken

There she sat, pretty as a bumble bee with her gold eyes and brown hair, attracting even more attention than the men with hydraulic grabs on building sites. She sat behind a sheet of plate glass in Dowbridge's window, at a desk that was all made of glass, and she had a mighty mirror behind her.

At her side was a dear little electric furnace, all in white, and on the desk was a guillotine; not the sort fed by tumbrils full of aristos, but a handy paper-cutting size. With this she was demolishing stacks and stacks of documents, cutting them into slivers like bacon, and then turning them round and repeating the process crossways until she had a mound of confetti. When it was knee-high she slid the whole heap into the plastic bucket and shot it into the furnace.

Pile after pile of paper the furnace wolfed down with the barest flicker of acknowledgment, and Roger Maul-everer, watching through the window, thought of pine forests in Sweden and Canada, vast stretches of spruce and redwood towering majestically in snow and sunshine, all destined to total extinction after this girl had done with them. He felt quite cross about it, for he liked trees. But he had to admit that the girl was very attractive.

Over her head, right across the plate glass, he could read the inscription:

CONFIDENTIAL RECORDS EFFECTIVELY
DESTROYED UNDER GUARANTEE.

The first two weeks Ghita Waring sat in the window, her boss, who had a flair for publicity, tied a bandage over her eyes so that it was plain she couldn't read the documents she was chopping. But she cut her finger three times.

The following week he put her in dark glasses, but he had to admit that the gold eyes were a loss. So the fourth week he contented himself with a notice in front of her desk:

SHE ONLY READS MUSIC;
YOUR SECRETS ARE SAFE WITH HER.

Ghita's old headmistress, who happened to pass by and see this, was very annoyed about it and complained that it was a poor advertisement for her school, but Ghita merely laughed and said she didn't mind; anyway it was almost true. Though she added that she could read cookery books if the words weren't too long. She managed to conceal her really dangerous gift; if it had been discovered she would hardly have landed the job.

It was a never-failing pleasure for passers-by to stop and watch her, and wonder what she was cutting up now.

'That's a will,' muttered Sidey Curtiss to Bill Brewer. 'Bang goes the long-lost blooming heir. Now what's she got?'

'Might be an agreement. See the red seal?'

'There goes a confidential file; some bloke's past history smoking up the chimbley. Pity she couldn't chop up your record, Bill, eh? Just phone police headquarters and tell 'em to send it along in a plain van.'

Bill took this bit of humour coldly. 'Why not ask 'er to chop off your finger-prints while she's at it?'

A van drew up beside them; not a plain one. It was one of Pickering and Pumphrey's expensive-looking utilities. Beside the driver sat Miss Inglis, the gaunt, severe secretary of old Mr Pumphrey himself. She got out of the van with dignity and marched inside, carrying a large roll of paper. She talked for a short time with the golden-eyed girl at the desk and then came out again, leaving the document behind her. She stepped back into the van and was buzzed away down to the immense and gleaming new office-building that Pickering and Pumphrey had just erected at the other end of the square.

'Wonder what they're getting rid of?' speculated Sidey.

'Something old Pumphrey doesn't want to be black-mailed about,' suggested Bill. 'Cor, here comes a smasher.' He stared approvingly at a sapphire-and-mink blonde who burst out of a taxi like a ray of sunshine coming out of a cloud. 'Bet *she's* got some com-promising letters.'

The blonde sailed inside, and presently the two watch-ers saw her pull a bundle of letters from her magnificent handbag and pass them across to the girl at the desk. They saw her talking vigorously.

'It really does seem a shame to destroy them,' was what she was saying. 'They're so romantic. I can't bear for someone not to see them. You read them, ducky. You must get bored chopping away all the time and never a chance of a peep. And Roger's letters are as good as Shakespeare; they're so poetic they always make me cry. It's like murdering a child to have them guillotined.' She dabbed at her eyes. 'But he says I've got to. See, in the last letter.'

Ghita looked at the top one. *Dear Rosemary*, it said baldly, *in view of developments, please destroy all my letters. I am returning yours herewith.*

'That's not very poetic, surely,' Ghita said.

'Ah, but look at the earlier ones, ducky.'

It certainly was rather a treat for Ghita to be allowed to read a document before destroying it, and she glanced at one or two of the letters towards the bottom of the pile. When she read them her golden eyes became larger and rounder and mistier.

'Why, they're beautiful,' she breathed.

'Aren't they?' said Rosemary with satisfaction. 'I do miss him, you know. No one else has ever said such beautiful things to me.' She dabbed her eyes again. 'Oh, would you mind giving me a testimonial, or whatever you call it, saying you've destroyed them? Roger is so fierce, and he's been beastly enough to me as it is. I don't want any more trouble,' her lips quivered.

The man must be a brute, Ghita thought indignantly. Fancy writing letters like that to a girl, and then making her destroy them; demanding it so curtly, too.

I hereby certify, she wrote, *that I have destroyed twenty hand-written letters to Miss Rosemary Trench-Giddering from 'Roger', Quincetree Cottage, Broken End, Hazeldean.*

Why, she thought to herself in sudden enlightenment, he must be the young architect that Mother's always talking about, who's taken Quincetree Cottage. I shouldn't have thought he'd been there long enough to write twenty letters. And then he asks her to destroy them. What a trifler! What a snake in the grass!

'That will be £1, please,' she said.

'Thank you, ducky,' said Rosemary. She gave a last dab to her eyes, a lingering glance at the last letter coming under the headsman's axe. 'Ah well . . .' She straightened her shoulders with a billowing glitter of mink, dazzled Ghita with her smile, and ran out to the taxi, which was still stolidly ticking up three pences.

'Now 'e won't be able ter prove a thing,' muttered Sidey to Bill. The drama had gone out of the window, but they still lingered in the spring sunshine watching Ghita, who had pulled towards her the large scroll left by Miss Inglis.

Absently she scanned it, and then blushed pink as she realised that she had violated professional ethics. Being allowed to read Rosemary's letters had led her astray.

She glanced up, scowled at the two seedy watchers outside, and grabbed her guillotine. In her confusion she let the scroll slip and it rolled to the floor, displaying its contents. She pounced on it and minced it into ribbons as if it had bitten her. Anyway it was only a blueprint; no possible harm could come from her having glanced at it.

'Did you see what that was?' said Bill to Sidey. 'It was the plans of Pickering and Pumphrey's new office building.'

'Well, what of it?' said Sidey. 'Come on, I'm getting cold. I want a cuppa.'

'What of it, you daft fool, what *of* it?? Why don't you see . . .'

He was talking urgently as they moved off to the Bide-Awhile Café.

It was bad luck on Ghita that she had a photographic memory.

'Some people are coming in for drinks,' Mrs Waring said when Ghita went home on Friday. 'That nice young Mr Mauleverer who's taken Quincetree Cottage will be here. I think I've mentioned him before.'

'Only about forty times,' said Ghita, but she said it to herself. She knew, and her mother knew that she knew, and she knew that her mother knew that she knew, that Mrs Waring disapproved of Ghita's chopping documents by day in order to put herself through music school at night. Both these occupations were nonsensical, Mrs Waring considered; the sort of fandangle that a girl who was engaged, say to a nice young architect, would soon put behind her.

Nice young Mr Mauleverer indeed, Ghita thought, hugging her mother affectionately. I could tell you a thing or two about that two-faced fiend in human form if I weren't a model of professional discretion. Just don't let him try his come-hither tactics on me, that's all.

Nice young Mr Mauleverer had a somewhat familiar face. After a little thought Ghita identified him as the tall, dark young man who had passed by her shop window nine or ten or eleven times in the course of the last few days. So that's who you are, is it, she thought, and she gave him such a flash of her eye, along with one of her mother's walnut canapés, that he staggered as if he had been stabbed with an eighteen-carat tiepin.

'I hear you are studying music,' he said, recovering. 'I compose a little myself.'

'Oh, do you?' Ghita said, interested in spite of herself. 'What sort of things?'

'Songs,' Roger Mauleverer said, and for some mysterious reason he chuckled. 'I write songs.'

The chuckle incensed Ghita. 'I shouldn't think you have a great deal of time for writing songs,' she said icily. 'Writing letters must be such an engrossing occupation.' She gave him a meaning look, and he eyed her warily.

'Am I to infer that my ex-fiancée has been to you professionally?'

'Miss Trench-Giddering has confided in me and has all my sympathy. But my lips are sealed,' Ghita said firmly. And that's settled *him*, she thought with satisfaction. Now we know where we stand with one another.

She darted another disapproving, golden flash at him;
was pleased to see that it appeared to leave him quite
prostrated; and went on to offer her walnut canapés
with the utmost grace and charm to ninety-years-old
Great Uncle Wilberforce.

On Wednesday, when Ghita was having her elevenses
over the local paper, in between spells of guillotining, her
satisfaction was given a jolt, and she was more than a
little disconcerted to read a report of the wedding of Miss
Rosemary Trench-Giddering to Mr Cecil Quayle, M.P.,
with eight bridesmaids and all the trimmings. There
were several photographs, and it was easy to see that Mr
Quayle, prosperous though he seemed—and as Ghita
knew him to be, for he owned the town's largest factory
—was about three times the age of the bride, who could
hardly be seen behind the enormous diamond she wore.

Ghita began to feel a little contrite and remorseful.
Lifting her eyes to the window she thought that supposing, just supposing, Roger Mauleverer were to pass by,
as he had done some eight or nine or ten times in the last
few days, there would be no harm in giving him a friendly smile. But there was nobody outside the window except
those two seedy-looking toughs who seemed to have spent
a lot of time loitering round there lately.

She turned back to the paper and a familiar name
caught her eye: Roger Mauleverer, A.R.I.B.A.

Roger Mauleverer, A.R.I.B.A., was, it appeared, the
architect responsible for the large new office building
recently erected in the town's main square on behalf of
the local firm of Pickering and Pumphrey; the building
had just been completed and the ceremonial tape cut by
Mrs Pumphrey, wife of the Managing Director.

An unusual feature of the building was the hidden
safe-deposit room concealed on one of its nine floors. No

one knew the whereabouts of this soundproof room
except Mr Pumphrey, Mr Harris the chief cashier and
the architect himself. Even the plans of the building had
been destroyed so that unauthorised persons could not
stumble on the information. The door of the room was
opened by the newest form of electronic device; it would
respond only to a code word that would open the door.

What ought she to do? Hasten to Mr Pumphrey and
tell him that his secret was discovered? Consult a psy-
chiatrist and ask if there was any way of expunging the
guilty knowledge from her mind? Or go to Roger
Mauleverer and ask his advice?

Something about the simplicity of the last course com-
mended itself. I'll ask him on Saturday, she thought—
for her mother had artlessly invited him to Saturday
supper. Nothing much can happen between now and
then.

She was very, very wrong.

If she had read the Stop Press column in the evening
paper, she would have seen the item headed, MISSING
MANAGING DIRECTOR. But she did not. She had a
class on Diminished and Augmented Triads at half past
six, and, hellbent to get to it, she thrust the evening
paper in among her shopping and ran like a doe to the
City Literary Institute in Tennyson Street.

It was late when she came out; late and dark and
quiet. Tennyson Street, all foggy and cobbled, looked
like a set from a French film, and it looked like it still
more when two shadowy figures came up softly and
menacingly behind Ghita and slipped a sack over her
head. Her hands were tied behind her back and she was
whisked into an alley that led, as she knew, to the river.

'Don't yell, *don't,*' a hoarse voice said warningly in her

ear, 'because if you do we'll have to treat you rough. Just you keep quiet. We only want you to tell us something and then we'll let you go.'

'What do you want?' Ghita gasped inside the bag. A cold premonition had already told her the answer.

'We was watching you the other day a-reading of a blueprint,' the voice said ingratiatingly. 'We saw your beautiful eyes a-taking of it in. All we want from you is the whereabouts of that there famous secret room at Pickering's what's got a million of di'monds shut away in it; and the code word for opening the door. That's all we want.'

'I shan't tell you,' said Ghita.

'Now, duck, don't you be so hasty. If you do tell us, who's to know it was you passed on the information? No one but us knows you read the plan. But if you don't tell us—'

'What?' Ghita said uneasily, for he had paused.

'Why, then I'm afraid we shall have to take you to the end of this alley and drop you in the river. Runs powerful fast the river does hereabouts,' the voice said reflectively.

Ghita shivered. She had never tried swimming with her hands tied behind her back, but she didn't think she would excel at it.

An idea struck her. 'I can't possibly explain where the door is,' she said. 'It's much too complicated. I can tell you the password. It's Lancashire Hot-Pot. Now will you let me go?'

'Not likely,' said Sidey. 'You'll have to come with us and show us. Once you get inside the building you'll know where you are. Coming? Or do we have to drop you in the water?'

'All right, I'm coming,' Ghita said sadly. 'The room's in the basement.'

The route they took to Pickering and Pumphrey's was circuitous, and entailed climbing some fences, crossing a bomb site, and cutting through a warehouse. At length they arrived in a wide, dark basement area next to a car park. Sidey, scouting ahead, picked a lock and let them in a service door.

Ghita saw nothing of all this, for her head was still in the sack, but now they took it off and let her look round and get her bearings. Unerringly she led them along a red-and-white tiled corridor in which floated a haunting and evocative smell of stew. It ended at double red doors, chromium handled, and labelled, DIRECTORS' CAN-TEEN. They were locked.

'Here you are,' Ghita whispered. 'That notice is a blind. It isn't really the canteen, that's on the first floor. Now you must stand here and say Lancashire Hot-Pot. But you have to say it in a particular tone of voice, and that's what I don't know, because I only saw it written down. You'll have to keep on trying till you hit the right pitch.'

'Got it all pat, ain't she,' Bill whispered admiringly. 'You oughter come into the profession, miss; you'd do champion at it. Now then, Sidey, you try first, tenor and counter-tenor. Then I'll try bass and baritone.'

At about the twentieth attempt, when they were getting really enthusiastic, Ghita slipped quietly away round the corner to the little block where LIFTS had been marked on the ground-plan.

Yes, here they were; and in such a modern building they were sure to be automatic. She pressed a button. Luckily they'd had to untie her hands to climb the fences. A lift came gliding down, and she tiptoed in and wafted herself up to the ninth floor where, among other things, she remembered having noticed the switchboard room. Thank goodness, the police station was only a couple of blocks away!

But when she stepped out of the lift she was thunderstruck to find lights burning, footsteps clattering and an atmosphere of hectic activity, very unexpected in an office building at ten minutes to midnight.

Three men hurried past her, distraught and preoccupied.

'Hey!' Ghita said. 'There are two burglars in the basement, trying to get into the safe-deposit room.'

'Those aren't burglars, my good girl,' one of the men said testily. 'The building's full of 'em. The Managing Director's got himself stuck inside the strongroom and no one knows where it is. Everybody's trying to find him.' Evidently he took her for a member of the staff.

'What about Mr Harris, the chief cashier?' suggested Ghita, very much taken aback by this new development.

'He's having his spring week sailing in the Baltic.'

'Well then, what about . . .'

But they hurried away, calling, 'Throgmorton, Throgmorton, have you tried the mezzanine floor?'

'Wait!' Ghita called. She chased them and caught them at the head of the stairs. 'I can tell you where the safe-deposit room is!'

'*You* can?' They turned and regarded her with suspicion. 'How?'

'Well, never mind that for now,' Ghita said. 'It's on this floor, the fourth door to the right from the auditor's room.'

By this time a group had assembled.

'I tried to get the architect, Mr Throgmorton,' someone panted. 'I tried five times. But there's no reply from his number.'

'This young person seems to think she knows where the door is,' Mr Throgmorton said with awful majesty.

Ghita's feelings of guilt and confusion intensified. She

went tremblingly up to the fourth door and pointed at it. 'That should be the one, and the password's Pickled Pumpkins.'

Mr Throgmorton gave her a look which, although she was ice-cold with fright, chilled her still further. He placed himself directly in front of the door, looked at it commandingly, and uttered the words, Pickled Pumpkins, in a sonorous voice.

Nothing happened.

Ghita began to wish that she could fall down the lift-shaft, or, failing that, just drop dead. She wondered what had gone wrong. And now that her password had failed, how was she ever going to introduce the topic of the two safe-breakers in the basement? But at that moment, she noticed that Roger Mauleverer was behind her.

'Ah, Mr Mauleverer,' Throgmorton said reprovingly. 'It took you a very long time to get here.'

'Long time?' Roger said, puzzled. 'I came just as fast as I possibly could. Is Miss Waring all right?' He looked anxiously at Ghita.

'Miss Waring? I am not aware that she has been in any trouble. It is Mr Pumphrey we are concerned with. Mr Pumphrey is immured in the strongroom.'

'Oh, is that all?' Roger said cheerfully. 'We can soon get him out of there.'

He stepped up to the door and serenaded it in a pleasing tenor.

> 'Safe, my dear, list and hear!
> None but I is standing near.'

This seemed an inaccuracy to Ghita, but everybody else was dead serious.

> 'None can pry, none can see,
> Open wide your door to me.'

The door swung open and revealed Mr Pumphrey, indignant and ravenous, ensconced in a nest of diamonds and securities.

'I forgot the tune,' he said accusingly to Roger. 'That's the trouble with these fancy gimmicks!'

'Well, sir,' said Roger, 'it was your idea to have a tune. If you recall, I was in favour of the simple words Pickled Pumpkins, and it was you who said that you'd look like a fool if one of your staff found you in the corridor saying Pickled Pumpkins, and it would be better if you had a verse that you could sing.'

· 'You must think of something else tomorrow,' snapped Mr Pumphrey. 'Have to, anyway, now half the staff's heard it.'

He glared round, explosive as a turkeycock. 'Let alone this young lady who's not a staff member. What's she doing here?'

'She told us where the strongroom was,' Throgmorton said.

'What? How the devil did she know that?'

Tremblingly, Ghita confessed how she had come by her knowledge.

'I shall ring up Dowbridge's,' Mr Pumphrey said, with the quiet menace of an impending avalanche. 'That's the last of my business they handle. And what, pray, were you doing in my building at this time of night?'

'I was b-brought here by two burglars,' Ghita faltered. 'They're down in the basement saying L-Lancashire Hot-Pot outside the Directors' Canteen.'

'I beg your pardon?'

But, thank heaven, Roger seemed to have grasped the situation. He murmured something to Throgmorton and the other two men. They shot away in the lift, found Sidey and Bill trying Hot-Pot for the seventy-seventh time in A alt and middle C, and nobbled them. The two burglars, hoarse and exhausted, were glad to go quietly.

'Where is Miss Waring?' Roger asked, when they led the captives before Mr Pumphrey, who had the telephone in his hand.

'She took her departure,' Mr Pumphrey said severely, 'after I had issued her a warning.' He put down the receiver.

Poor Ghita crept to her office next morning more dead than alive. Instead of the usual pile of documents awaiting destruction there was one envelope on her desk. It said, *Please read before destroying.* Inside was a week's salary and notice of dismissal from her boss, who had been rung by Mr Pumphrey at ten minutes past midnight.

Two large tears trickled down Ghita's cheeks and splashed on the glass desk. Absently she slid her notice into the guillotine and sliced it into spills. Then she looked up and saw Roger outside the window. She glared at him. Undeterred, he came in.

'It's all your fault,' Ghita stormed at him. 'If I hadn't been inveigled into reading your letters I'd never have looked at that blueprint. And now I've got the sack, and I'll probably go to p-prison, and I'll never be able to afford to finish learning about Diminished and Augmented Triads, and what do *you* care?'

'I do care,' Roger said. 'Very much. I *love* Augmented Triads.' Something about the way in which he said this, coupled with the fact that he was holding Ghita in a close embrace at the time, carried instant conviction.

He went on, 'I explained to Mr Pumphrey that you'd been shanghai'd, and he says he's sorry he misunderstood the situation and he'll put it right with your boss.'

'But how did you know about it?' Ghita said, wiping

her eyes on his lapel, regardless of the interested spectators outside.

'I was lecturing on architecture at the City Literary
Institute last night, and I looked out of the window and
saw them putting your head in the bag. By the time I'd
dashed out you were gone, but I guessed where they'd
be making for.'

'It was nice of you to bother,' Ghita said, and added
in a small voice, 'I owe you an apology about Miss
Trench-Giddering. Did you mind terribly when she
married Mr Quayle?'

'Frankly, no,' said Roger, very cheerfully for a rejected
suitor. 'She was grand for practising my literary style on.
But I wouldn't want to spend my life with somebody who
sleeps all day and spends the hours between ten p.m. and
five a.m. in half a dozen night clubs. I hate ear-splitting
music.'

Ghita drew back a couple of inches and looked at him
nervously.

'What about piano-playing?'

'The minute we're married,' he said, 'I shall design us
a house with a soundproof room in the middle, where
you can pile up the Augmented Triads to your heart's
content.'

The Advantages of Cheese as a Travelling Companion

by Jerome K. Jerome

I remember a friend of mine buying a couple of cheeses at Liverpool. Splendid cheeses they were, ripe and mellow, and with a two hundred horsepower scent about them that might have been warranted to carry three miles, and knock a man over at two hundred yards. I was in Liverpool at the time, and my friend said that if I didn't mind he would get me to take them back to London, as he should not be coming up for a day or two himself, and he did not think the cheeses ought to be kept much longer.

'Oh, with pleasure, dear boy,' I replied, 'with pleasure.'

I called for the cheeses, and took them away in a cab. It was a ramshackle affair, dragged along by a knock-kneed, broken-winded somnambulist, which his owner, in a moment of enthusiasm, during conversation, referred to as a horse. I put the cheeses on the top, and we started off at a shamble that would have done credit to the swiftest steam roller ever built, and all went merry as a funeral bell, until we turned a corner. There, the wind carried a whiff from the cheeses full on our steed. It woke him up, and, with a snort of terror, he dashed off at three miles an hour. The wind still blew in his direction, and before we reached the end of the street he was laying himself out at the rate of nearly four miles an hour, leaving the cripples and stout old ladies simply nowhere.

It took two porters as well as the driver to hold him at the station; and I do not think they would have done it, even then, had not one of the men had the presence of mind to put a handkerchief over his nose, and to light a bit of brown paper.

I took my ticket, and marched proudly up the platform, with my cheeses, the people falling back respectfully on either side. The train was crowded, and I had to get into a carriage where there were already seven other people. One crusty old gentleman objected, but I got in, notwithstanding; and, putting my cheeses upon the rack, squeezed down with a pleasant smile, and said it was a warm day. A few moments passed, and then the old gentleman began to fidget.

'Very close in here,' he said.

'Quite oppressive,' said the man next to him.

And then they both began sniffing, and, at the third sniff, they caught it right on the chest, and rose up without another word and went out. And then a stout lady got up, and said it was disgraceful that a respectable married woman should be harried about in this way, and gathered up a bag and eight parcels and went. The remaining four passengers sat on for a while, until a solemn-looking man in the corner who, from his dress and general appearance, seemed to belong to the undertaker class, said it put him in mind of a dead baby; and the other three passengers tried to get out of the door at the same time, and hurt themselves.

I smiled at the black gentleman, and said I thought we were going to have the carriage to ourselves; and he laughed pleasantly and said that some people made such a fuss over a little thing. But even he grew strangely depressed after we had started, and so, when we reached Crewe, I asked him to come and have a drink. He accepted, and we forced our way into the buffet, where we yelled, and stamped, and waved our umbrellas for a quarter of an hour; and then a young lady came and asked us if we wanted anything.

'What's yours?' I said, turning to my friend.

'I'll have half-a-crown's worth of brandy, neat, if you please, miss,' he responded.

And he went off quietly after he had drunk it and got into another carriage, which I thought mean.

From Crewe I had the compartment to myself, though the train was crowded. As we drew up at the different stations, the people, seeing my empty carriage, would rush for it. 'Here y'are, Maria; come along, plenty of room.' 'All right, Tom; we'll get in here,' they would shout. And they would run along, carrying heavy bags, and fight round the door to get in first. And one would open the door and mount the steps and stagger back into the arms of the man behind him; and they would all come and have a sniff, and then drop off and squeeze into other carriages, or pay the difference and go First.

From Euston I took the cheeses down to my friend's house. When his wife came into the room she smelt round for an instant. Then she said:

'What is it? Tell me the worst.'

I said:

'It's cheeses. Tom bought them in Liverpool, and asked me to bring them up with me.'

And I added that I hoped she understood that it had nothing to do with me; and she said that she was sure of that, but that she would speak to Tom about it when he came back.

My friend was detained in Liverpool longer than he

expected; and three days later as he hadn't returned home, his wife called on me. She said:

'What did Tom say about those cheeses?'

I replied that he had directed they were to be kept in a moist place, and that nobody was to touch them.

She said:

'Nobody's likely to touch them. Had he smelt them?'

I thought he had, and added that he seemed greatly attached to them.

'You think he would be upset,' she queried, 'if I gave a man a sovereign to take them away and bury them?'

I answered that I thought he would never smile again.

An idea struck her. She said:

'Do you mind keeping them for him? Let me send them round to you.'

'Madam,' I replied, 'for myself I like the smell of cheese, and the journey the other day with them from Liverpool I shall ever look back upon as a happy ending to a pleasant holiday. But, in this world, we must consider others. The lady under whose roof I have the honour of residing is a widow, and, for all I know, possibly an orphan too. She has a strong, I may say an eloquent, objection to being what she terms "put upon". The presence of your husband's cheese in her house she would, I instinctively feel, regard as a "put upon"; and it shall never be said that I put upon the widow and the orphan.'

'Very well, then,' said my friend's wife, rising, 'all I have to say is, that I shall take the children and go to an hotel until those cheeses are eaten. I decline to live any longer in the same house with them.'

She kept her word, leaving the place in charge of the charwoman, who, when asked if she could stand the smell, replied: 'What smell?' and who, when taken close to the cheeses and told to sniff hard, said she could detect a faint odour of melons. It was argued from this that little injury could result to the woman from the atmosphere, and she was left.

The hotel bill came to fifteen guineas; and my friend, after reckoning everything up, found that the cheeses had cost him eight-and-sixpence a pound. He said he dearly loved a bit of cheese, but it was beyond his means; so he determined to get rid of them. He threw them into the canal; but had to fish them out again, as the bargemen complained. They said it made them feel quite faint. And, after that, he took them one dark night and left them in the parish mortuary. But the coroner discovered them, and made a fearful fuss.

He said it was a plot to deprive him of his living by waking up the corpses.

My friend got rid of them, at last, by taking them down to a seaside town, and burying them on the beach. It gained the place quite a reputation. Visitors said they had never noticed before how strong the air was, and weak-chested and consumptive people used to throng there for years afterwards.

FROM *Three Men in a Boat*

The Scholarly Mouse

by Dal Stivens

A studious young mouse immersed himself in his books and then declared in the presence of an ancient:

'I have found the way to the millennium!'

The aged mouse wiped a rheumy eye before replying scornfully, 'Everyone knows the way—we've known it for centuries—but no one yet has found a way of belling the cat.'

'Crude and unscientific!' said the studious young mouse. 'Hypnotism is the lurk.'

'All my eye!' said the old mouse. 'Hypnotise me—or whatever the verb is—'

The young mouse made a few passes with his right paw and left the ancient chewing a bit of soap under the delusion it was prize Limburger. He set his shoulders, made his way along the inside of the skirting-board, emerged from the hole and marched forthrightly across the carpet to where the ginger cat was sleeping by the fire.

When the mouse was about ten feet short the cat awoke. He blinked at the sight of the mouse coming on boldly towards him and told himself:

'I must be still dreaming! Obviously that last mouse was too much for me.'

'So will this one be!' said the studious young mouse in a resolute voice.

The cat sat up with a jerk then.

'You'll pardon the question, I hope,' he said silkily, 'but have I perhaps bitten you behind the ears on the occasion of an earlier meeting?'

'No,' said the mouse in a stern voice, still coming on.

'Extr'ordinary!' said the ginger cat. He shrugged his shoulders. 'Who am I to argue with my supper?'

The mouse concentrated hard, gathered the corners of his lids together until his eyes glittered like those of a villain in a Victorian melodrama, and made a couple of passes with his right paw, saying, 'Cat, you're very sleepy. You're very sleepy. You're very sleepy.'

'Oh, but I'm not a bit sl—' the cat started to say and then yawned.

'You see in front of you a large fierce dog!' said the mouse.

'By Gad, I believe you're right!' said the cat to himself. 'Extr'ordinary! Fierce, too!' His fur flew up on the back of his neck and he shook with fear. He went up four feet in the air, fell over on his back with funk, mizzled out the door, out of the house and kept on going.

The young mouse's triumph was complete and the other mice in the house proclaimed him the saviour of their race; quite soon his fame had spread to other households where mice sought his help.

'I must help them,' said the young mouse. 'The good life is the right of all members of our race.'

He gave tirelessly of his services and liberated first whole streets and then whole suburbs.

Meanwhile, the ginger cat was in a cats' home and explaining his neurosis to other refugees:

'I could have sworn it was a mouse and then, by Gad, it was a mastiff with teeth as big as butchers' knives.'

'My experience was the same except it was an Alsatian,' said a tabby.

'An Irish wolfhound made me a displaced person!' said a Persian. 'I had the finest home in the world.'

'A bull-terrier frightened me out of seven of my lives,' said a tortoiseshell.

'A greyhound flummoxed me out of eight and a half,' said a black cat, weakly.

An albino cat, who had been listening to the conversation, now contributed:

'One common factor is that all of us saw, or thought we saw, a mouse, in the first place. It appears to me that some form of mass hysteria is at work.'

'Who's hysterical, by Gad?' cried the ginger cat.

'I'm the same as the next cat!' shouted the tabby.

'It's you that's hysterical!' cried the Persian to the albino.

'You read too much!' shouted the tortoiseshell. 'All that silly psychology stuff!'

'As you wish, gentlemen and idiots,' said the albino. 'I was trying to help. However, I see I must do it alone. I'm going back to beard the mastiff, the Alsatian, the Irish wolfhound, the bull-terrier, the greyhound—to say nothing of my own timber-wolf which I saw at dusk. Good afternoon, fellow psychotics!'

Outside in the street, however, the albino cat did not feel so brave, particularly as the afternoon sun blinded him. He bumped into lamp-posts and garbage tins, fell into gutters, tripped over stones and once narrowly escaped being run down by an animal ambulance with a load of hysterical cats.

'Those dolts at the home are more blind than I am!' the albino cat told himself and pressed on, resolutely.

In the late afternoon he drew near his former home. He was drawing a couple of deep breaths before entering when he caught the whiff of a mouse. It was the studious young mouse returning from extending the mouse millennium to another household.

'Just a moment, mouse,' said the albino cat, groping forward.

'One I've missed,' said the young mouse, under his breath. Aloud, he said, 'You're very sleepy. You're very sleepy. You're very sleepy.'

'I am rather,' said the albino cat. 'I've come miles and I'm in a bad temper—all because of those ignorant fools back in the cats' home. No progress will ever be made while members of our race despise study and sneer at book learning.'

'You see in front of you a big fierce dog!' said the mouse.

'Not a thing,' said the albino cat. 'As I was saying, it is a few choice spirits that are responsible for all the progress which is made in the world—'

'A big fierce dog!' repeated the mouse. He waved his paws excitedly and repeated, 'A big fierce dog!' coming to within a few inches of the cat.

'Eureka!' cried the albino cat. 'I've got it! I'm damned, a mouse that practises hypnotism!' He put out a paw and trapped the mouse. 'I wish I could see you, my friend. You're a choice spirit like myself.'

'Can't see me!' gasped the mouse. 'Oh, I'm undone!'

'I'm afraid so,' said the albino cat. 'Can't see a thing till the sun gets down.' He went on tenderly, 'I could love you, my friend, if Nature hadn't ruled otherwise.' He started to laugh. 'To think of how you fooled those idiots, that pompous ginger cat, the silly Persian, and the rest—I have it! I'll keep you round for a while.' He bit the mouse behind the ears. 'You can keep on scaring them, on my orders.'

'As you wish,' said the mouse, playing for time, though

he knew his was now short. And he told himself, 'One last effort for my race.'

At nine o'clock that evening a screaming hysterical albino cat was returned to the home. His eyes were leaping from his head and he cried, 'Such a dog! It had three heads—one a timber-wolf's, the middle one a mastiff's and the other an Irish wolfhound's! It had two mouths on each head and three rows of teeth and—'

'Extr'ordinary performance!' said the ginger cat.

'Look where his psychology has got him,' said the tortoiseshell.

FROM *The Scholarly Mouse and Other Tales*

Tobias the Terrible

by Damon Runyon

One night I am sitting in Mindy's restaurant on Broadway partaking heartily of some Hungarian goulash which comes very nice in Mindy's, what with the chef being personally somewhat Hungarian himself, when in pops a guy who is a stranger to me and sits down at my table.

I do not pay any attention to the guy at first as I am busy looking over the entries for the next day at Laurel, but I hear him tell the waiter to bring him some goulash, too. By and by I hear the guy making a strange noise and I look at him over my paper and see that he is crying. In fact, large tears are rolling down his face into his goulash and going plop-plop as they fall.

Now it is by no means usual to see guys crying in Mindy's restaurant, though thousands of guys come in there who often feel like crying, especially after a tough day at the track, so I commence weighing the guy up with great interest. I can see he is a very little guy, maybe a shade over five feet high and weighing maybe as much as a dime's worth of liver, and he has a moustache like a mosquito's whiskers across his upper lip, and pale blond hair and a very sad look in his eyes.

Furthermore, he is a young guy and he is wearing a suit of clothes the colour of French mustard, with slanting pockets, and I notice when he comes in that he has a

132

brown hat sitting jack-deuce on his noggin. Anybody can see that this guy does not belong in these parts, with such a sad look and especially with such a hat.

Naturally, I figure his crying is some kind of a dodge. In fact, I figure that maybe the guy is trying to cry me out of the price of his Hungarian goulash, although if he takes the trouble to ask anybody before he comes in, he will learn that he may just as well try to cry Al Smith out of the Empire State Building.

But the guy does not say anything whatever to me but just goes on shedding tears into his goulash, and finally I get very curious about this proposition, and I speak to him as follows:

'Listen, pally,' I say, 'if you are crying about the goulash, you better dry your tears before the chef sees you, because,' I say, 'the chef is very sensitive about his goulash, and may take your tears as criticism.'

'The goulash seems all right,' the guy says in a voice that is just about his size. 'Anyway, I am not crying about the goulash. I am crying about my sad life. Friend,' the guys says, 'are you ever in love?'

Well, of course, at this crack I know what is eating the guy. If I have all the tears that are shed on Broadway by guys in love, I will have enough salt water to start an opposition ocean to the Atlantic and Pacific, with enough left over to run the Great Salt Lake out of business. But I wish to say I never shed any of these tears personally, because I am never in love, and furthermore, barring a bad break, I never expect to be in love, for the way I look at it love is strictly the old phedinkus, and I tell the little guy as much.

'Well,' he says, 'you will not speak so harshly of love if you are acquainted with Miss Deborah Weems.'

With this he starts crying more than somewhat, and his grief is such that it touches my heart and I have half a notion to start crying with him as I am now convinced that the guy is levelling with his tears.

Finally the guy slacks up a little in his crying, and begins eating his goulash, and by and by he seems more cheerful, but then it is well known to one and all that a fair dose of Mindy's goulash will cheer up anybody no matter how sad they feel. Pretty soon the guy starts talking to me, and I make out that his name is Tobias Tweeney, and that he comes from a spot over in Bucks County, Pennsylvania, by the name of Erasmus, or some such.

Furthermore, I judge that this Erasmus is not such a large city, but very pleasant, and that Tobias Tweeney is born and raised there and is never much of any place else in his life, although he is now rising twenty-five.

Well, it seems that Tobias Tweeney has a fine position in a shoe store selling shoes and is going along all right when he happens to fall in love with a doll by the name of Miss Deborah Weems, whose papa owns a gas station in Erasmus and is a very prominent citizen. I judge from what Tobias tells me that this Miss Deborah Weems tosses him around quite some, which proves to me that dolls in small towns are just the same as they are on Broadway.

'She is beautiful,' Tobias Tweeney says, speaking of Miss Deborah Weems. 'I do not think I can live without her. But,' he says, 'Miss Deborah Weems will have no part of me because she is daffy over desperate characters of the underworld such as she sees in the movies at the Model Theatre in Erasmus.

'She wishes to know,' Tobias Tweeney says, 'why I cannot be a big gunman and go around plugging people

here and there and talking up to politicians and policemen, and maybe looking picturesque and romantic like
Edward G. Robinson or James Cagney or even Georgie
Raft. But, of course,' Tobias says, 'I am not the type for
such a character. Anyway,' he says, 'Constable Wendell
will never permit me to be such a character in Erasmus.

'So Miss Deborah Weems says I have no more nerve
than a catfish,' Tobias says, 'and she goes around with a
guy by the name of Joe Trivett, who runs the Smoke
Shop, and bootlegs ginger extract to the boys in his back
room and claims Al Capone once says "Hello" to him,
although,' Tobias says, 'personally, I think Joe Trivett
is nothing but a great big liar.'

At this, Tobias Tweeney starts crying again, and I feel
very sorry for him indeed, because I can see he is a
friendly, harmless little fellow, and by no means accustomed to being tossed around by a doll, and a guy who
is not accustomed to being tossed around by a doll always
finds it most painful the first time.

'Why,' I say, very indignant, 'this Miss Deborah
Weems talks great foolishness, because big gunmen always wind up nowadays with the score nine to nought
against them, even in the movies. In fact,' I say, 'if they
do not wind up this way in the movies, the censors will
not permit the movies to be displayed. Why do you not
hit this guy Trivett a punch in the snoot,' I say, 'and tell
him to go about his business?'

'Well,' Tobias says, 'the reason I do not hit him a
punch in the snoot is because he has the idea of punching
snoots first, and whose snoot does he punch but mine.
Furthermore,' Tobias says, 'he makes my snoot bleed
with the punch, and he says he will do it again if I keep
hanging around Miss Deborah Weems. And,' Tobias
says, 'it is mainly because I do not return the punch,

being too busy stopping my snoot from bleeding, that Miss Deborah Weems renounces me for ever.

'She says she can never stand for a guy who has no more nerve than me,' Tobias says, 'but,' he says, 'I ask you if I am to blame if my mother is frightened by a rabbit a few weeks before I am born, and marks me for life?

'So I leave town,' Tobias says. 'I take my savings of two hundred dollars out of the Erasmus bank, and I come here, figuring maybe I will meet up with some big gunmen and other desperate characters of the underworld, and get to know them, and then I can go back to Erasmus and make Joe Trivett look sick. By the way,' he says, 'do you know any desperate characters of the underworld?'

Well, of course I do not know any such characters, and if I do know them I am not going to speak about it, because the best a guy can get in this town if he goes around speaking of these matters is a nice kick in the pants. So I say no to Tobias Tweeney, and tell him I am more or less of a stranger myself, and then he wishes to know if I can show him a tough joint, such as he sees in the movies.

Naturally, I do not know of such a joint, but then I get to thinking about Good Time Charley's little Gingham Shoppe over in Forty-seventh Street, and how Charley is not going so good the last time I am in there, and here is maybe a chance for me to steer a little trade his way, because, after all, guys with two yards in their pocket are by no means common nowadays.

So I take Tobias Tweeney around to Good Time Charley's, but the moment we get in there I am sorry we go, because who is present but a dozen parties from different parts of the city, and none of these parties are any bargain at any time. Some of these parties, such as Harry the Horse and Angie the Ox are from Brooklyn, and three are from Harlem, including Little Mitzi and Germany Schwartz, and several are from the Bronx, because I recognise Joey Uptown, and Joey never goes around without a few intimate friends from his own neighbourhood with him.

Afterwards I learn that these parties are to a meeting on business matters at a spot near Good Time Charley's, and when they get through with their business they drop in to give Charley a little complimentary play, for Charley stands very good with one and all in this town. Anyway, they are sitting around a table when Tobias Tweeney and I arrive, and I give them all a big hello, and they hello me back, and ask me and my friend to sit down as it seems they are in a most hospitable frame of mind.

Naturally I sit down because it is never good policy to decline an invitation from parties such as these, and I motion Tobias to sit down, too, and I introduce Tobias all around, and we all have a couple of drinks, and then I explain to those present just who Tobias is, and how his ever-loving doll tosses him around, and how Joe Trivett punches him in the snoot.

Well, Tobias begins crying again, because no inexperienced guy can take a couple of drinks of Good Time Charley's liquor and not bust out crying, even if it is Charley's company liquor, and one and all are at once very sympathetic with Tobias, especially Little Mitzi, who is just tossed around himself more than somewhat by a doll. In fact, Little Mitzi starts crying with him.

'Why,' Joey Uptown says, 'I never hear of a greater outrage in my life, although,' he says, 'I can see there is some puppy in you at that, when you do not return this

Trivett's punch. But even so,' Joey says, 'if I have time I will go back to this town you speak of with you and make the guy hard to catch. Furthermore,' he says, 'I will give this Deborah Weems a piece of my mind.'

Then I tell them how Tobias Tweeney comes to New York figuring he may meet up with some desperate characters of the underworld, and they hear this with great interest, and Angie the Ox speaks as follows:

'I wonder,' Angie says, 'if we can get in touch with anybody who knows such characters and arrange to have Mr Tweeney meet them, although personally,' Angie says, 'I loathe and despise characters of this nature.'

Well, while Angie is wondering this there comes a large knock at the front door, and it is such a knock as only the gendarmes can knock, and everybody at the table jumps up. Good Time Charley goes to the door and takes a quiet gander through his peephole and we hear a loud, coarse voice speaking as follows:

'Open up, Charley,' the voice says. 'We wish to look over your guests. Furthermore,' the voice says, 'tell them not to try the back door, because we are there, too.'

'It is Lieutenant Harrigan and his squad,' Charley says as he comes back to the table where we are all standing. 'Someone must tip him off you are here. Well,' Charley says, 'those who have rods to shed will shed them now.'

At this, Joey Uptown steps up to Tobias Tweeney and hands him a large Betsy and says to Tobias like this:

'Put this away on you somewhere,' Joey says, 'and then sit down and be quiet. These coppers are not apt to bother with you,' Joey says, 'if you sit still and mind your own business, but,' Joey says, 'it will be very tough on any of us they find with a rod, especially any of us who owe the state any time, and,' Joey says, 'I seem to remember I owe some.'

Now of course what Joey says is very true, because he is only walking around and about on parole, and some of the others present are walking around the same way, and it is a very serious matter for a guy who is walking around on parole to be caught with a John Roscoe in his pocket. So it is a very ticklish situation, and somewhat embarrassing.

Well, Tobias Tweeney is somewhat dazed by his couple of drinks of Good Time Charley's liquor and the chances are he does not realise what is coming off, so he takes Joey's rod and puts it in his hip kick. Then all of a sudden Harry the Horse and Angie the Ox and Little Mitzi, and all the others step up to him and hand him their Roscoes and Tobias Tweeney somehow manages to stow the guns away on himself and sit down before Good Time Charley opens the door and in come the gendarmes.

By this time Joey Uptown and all the others are scattered at different tables around the room, with no more than three at any one table, leaving Tobias Tweeney and me alone at the table where we are first sitting. Furthermore, everybody is looking very innocent indeed, and all hands seem somewhat surprised at the intrusion of the gendarmes, who are all young guys belonging to Harrigan's Broadway squad and very rude.

I know Harrigan by sight, and I know most of his men, and they know there is no more harm in me than there is in a two-year-old baby, so they pay no attention to me whatever, or to Tobias Tweeney, either, but go around making Joey Uptown, and Angie the Ox, and all the others stand up while the gendarmes fan them to see if they have any rods on them, because these gendarmes are always laying for parties such as these hoping to catch them rodded up.

Naturally the gendarmes do not find any rods on any-body, because the rods are all on Tobias Tweeney, and no gendarme is going to fan Tobias Tweeney looking for a rod after one gander at Tobias, especially at this parti-cular moment, as Tobias is now half-asleep from Good Time Charley's liquor, and has no interest whatever in anything that is going on. In fact, Tobias is nodding in his chair.

Of course the gendarmes are greatly disgusted at not finding any rods, and Angie the Ox and Joey Uptown are telling them that they are going to see their aldermen and find out if law-abiding citizens can be stood up and fanned for rods, and put in a very undignified position like this, but the gendarmes do not seem disturbed by these threats, and Lieutenant Harrigan states as follows:

'Well,' he says, 'I guess maybe I get a bum steer, but,' he says, 'for two cents I will give all you wrong gees a good going-over for luck.'

Of course this is no way to speak to parties such as these, as they are all very prominent in their different parts of the city, but Lieutenant Harrigan is a guy who seldom cares how he talks to anybody. In fact, Lieutenant Harrigan is a very tough copper.

But he is just about to take his gendarmes out of the joint when Tobias Tweeney nods a little too far forward in his chair, and then all of sudden topples over on the floor, and five large rods pop out of his pockets and go sliding every which way around the floor, and the next thing anybody knows there is Tobias Tweeney under arrest with all the gendarmes holding on to some part of him.

Well, the next day the newspapers are plumb full of the capture of a guy they call Twelve-Gun Tweeney, and the papers say the police state that this is undoubtedly the toughest guy the world ever sees, because while they hear of two-gun guys, and even three-gun guys, they never before hear of a guy going around rodded up with twelve guns.

The gendarmes say they can tell by the way he acts that Twelve-Gun Tweeney is a mighty bloodthirsty guy, because he says nothing whatever but only glares at them with a steely glint in his eyes, although of course the reason Tobias stares at them is because he is still too dumbfounded to think of anything to say.

Naturally, I figure that when Tobias comes up for air he is a sure thing to spill the whole business, and all the parties who are in Good Time Charley's when he is arrested figure the same way, and go into retirement for a time. But it seems that when Tobias finally realises what time it is, he is getting so much attention that it swells him all up and he decides to keep on being Twelve-Gun Tweeney as long as he can, which is a decision that is a very nice break for all parties concerned.

I sneak down to Judge Rascover's court the day Tobias is arraigned on a charge of violation of the Sullivan law, which is a law against carrying rods, and the courtroom is packed with citizens eager to see a character desperate enough to lug twelve rods, and among these citizens are many dolls, pulling and hauling for position, and some of these dolls are by no means crows. Many photographers are hanging around to take pictures of Twelve-Gun Tweeney as he is led in handcuffed to gendarmes on either side of him, and with other gendarmes in front and behind him.

But one and all are greatly surprised and somewhat disappointed when they see what a little squirt Tobias is, and Judge Rascover looks down at him once, and then puts on his specs and takes another gander as if he does not believe what he sees in the first place. After looking at Tobias awhile through his specs, and shaking his head as if he is greatly puzzled, Judge Rascover speaks to Lieutenant Harrigan as follows:

'Do you mean to tell this court,' Judge Rascover says, 'that this half-portion here is the desperate Twelve-Gun Tweeney?'

Well, Lieutenant Harrigan says there is no doubt whatever about it, and Judge Rascover wishes to know how Tobias carries all these rods, and whereabouts, so Lieutenant Harrigan collects twelve rods from the gendarmes around the courtroom, unloads these rods, and starts in putting the guns here and there on Tobias as near as he can remember where they are found on him in the first place, with Tobias giving him a little friendly assistance.

Lieutenant Harrigan puts two guns in each of the side pockets of Tobias's coat, one in each hip pocket, one in the waistband of Tobias's pants, one in each side pocket of the pants, one up each of Tobias's sleeves and one in the inside pocket of Tobias's coat. Then Lieutenant Harrigan states to the court that he is all finished, and that Tobias is rodded up in every respect as when they put the arm on him in Good Time Charley's joint, and Judge Rascover speaks to Tobias as follows:

'Step closer to the bench,' Judge Rascover says. 'I wish to see for myself just what kind of a villain you are.'

Well, Tobias takes a step forward, and over he goes on his snoot, so I see right away what it is makes him keel over in Good Time Charley's joint, not figuring in Charley's liquor. The little guy is just naturally top-heavy from the rods.

Now there is much confusion as he falls and a young doll who seems to be fatter than somewhat comes shoving through the crowd in the courtroom yelling and crying, and though the gendarmes try to stop her she gets to Tobias and kneels at his side, and speaks as follows:

'Toby, darling,' she says, 'it is nobody but Deborah, who loves you dearly, and who always knows you will turn out to be the greatest gunman of them all. Look at me, Toby,' she says, 'and tell me you love me, too. We never realise what a hero you are until we get the New York papers in Erasmus last night, and I hurry to you as quickly as possible. Kiss me, Toby,' the fat young doll says, and Tobias raises up on one elbow and does the same, and it makes a very pleasing scene, indeed, although the gendarmes try to pull them apart, having no patience whatever with such matters.

Now Judge Rascover is watching all this business through his specs, and Judge Rascover is no sucker, but a pretty slick old codger for a judge, and he can see that there is something wrong somewhere about Tobias Tweeney being a character as desperate as the gendarmes make him out, especially when he sees that Tobias cannot pack all these rods on a bet.

So when the gendarmes pick the fat young doll off of Tobias and take a few pounds of rods off of Tobias, too, so he is finally able to get back on his pins and stand there, Judge Rascover adjourns court, and takes Tobias into his private room and has a talk with him, and the chances are Tobias tells him the truth, for the next thing anybody knows Tobias is walking away as free as the little birdies in the trees, except that he has the fat young doll clinging to him like a porous plaster, so maybe Tobias is not so free, at that.

Well, this is about all there is to the story, except that there is afterwards plenty of heat between the parties who are present in Good Time Charley's joint when

Tobias is collared, because it seems that the meeting they all attend before going to Charley's is supposed to be a peace meeting of some kind and nobody is supposed to carry any rods to this meeting just to prove their confidence in each other, so everybody is very indignant when it comes out that nobody has any confidence in anybody else at the meeting.

I never hear of Tobias Tweeney but once after all this, and it is some months afterwards when Joey Uptown and Little Mitzi are over in Pennsylvania inspecting a brewery proposition, and finding themselves near the town that is called Erasmus, they decide it will be a nice thing to drop in on Tobias Tweeney and see how he is getting along.

Well, it seems Tobias is all married up to Miss Deborah Weems, and is getting along first class, as it seems the town elects him constable, because it feels that a guy with such a desperate reputation as Tobias Tweeney's is bound to make wrongdoers keep away from Erasmus if he is an officer of the law, and Tobias's first official act is to chase Joe Trivett out of town.

But along Broadway Tobias Tweeney will always be considered nothing but an ingrate for heaving Joey Uptown and Little Mitzi into the town sneezer and getting them fined fifty bobs apiece for carrying concealed weapons.   FROM *More than Somewhat*

'The lamps are going out all over Europe'

(Edward, Viscount Grey of Falloden, August 3, 1914)

by Frank Muir

Those familiar with the B.B.C. panel game My Word *know that at the end of the programme Frank Muir and Denis Norden compete to offer the most unlikely explanation of how a famous quotation originated. The result is usually a pun so awful as to be almost unrecognisable.*

The Most Unforgettable Character I ever met was—well, he's dead now and I don't remember much about him. On the other hand, the Most Forgettable Character I ever met is most memorable. He was elected Most Forgettable Character by our form at school. The craze for electing the Most Something-or-other had hit our form heavily that year—I was, I recall, elected the Most Smelly, an injustice which has rankled ever since. But the application of the word 'forgettable' to Oliver Sinclair Yarrop was only too appropriate. I can see him now, a veal-faced lad with no colour about him anywhere; his hair was the same colour as his skin, which was colourless; he had almost transparent ears. He took no interest at all in the normal pursuits of healthy schoolboys, like boasting loudly, spitting, eating, punching girls: his sole passion in life was the love, and care, of animals.

It is a melancholy fact, which as schoolboys we but dimly perceived, that Dame Fate is a cruel Jade; and one of her little caprices is to allow a growing lad to work up a lifetime ambition whilst at the same time making sure that he is totally unequipped to achieve it. Thus my best friend, Nigel Leatherbarrow, wanted to be the Pope: he was Jewish. And my second-best-friend, Tarquin Wilson, wanted to be a girl. And I wanted to be rich. But the worst example was poor little, Forgettable Oliver; he desperately wanted to be a vet, and much as he loved animals, they loathed him.

I, interested in people but indifferent to furred and feathered beasts, was beloved by the animal kingdom. Even now I cannot walk very far before dogs appear from nowhere and sniff my socks. When I return home I find a nest of field mice in my turn-ups. I have only to pause a moment to lean up against a tree and ladybirds settle on me in such numbers that I look as if I have galloping chicken pox.

But all animal life viewed Oliver with implacable hatred. Full of love for them, he would hold out his left hand for every dog to sniff. When he left school the fingers of his left hand were an inch shorter than those of his right hand. Every pullover he possessed was lacerated by kittens' claws. One of his jackets had lost a shoulder where a cow had taken a bite at him. His right shin bore a scar where a chicken had driven her beak in. Animals had bitten him so much that when I saw him, for the last time, stripped for gym, he looked deckle-edged.

I did not see Oliver again until after the war. I was at an RAF hospital in the country being treated for shock

—brought on by the realisation that I was about to be demobilised and would have to work for a living—and on a country walk I suddenly came upon Oliver. He had his back to a brick wall and was being attacked by a duckling. Unclamping the bird's beak from Oliver's ankle, I fell to talking. He had changed considerably since we had last met. He no longer wore his school cap, and long trousers covered his bony, unmemorable knees. He seemed middle-aged before his time. He had on one of those gingery, very thick tweed suits with bits in them which look as though they had been woven from marmalade. His hair was very thin; almost emaciated. And he only had one arm.

It seems that he gave up all hopes of becoming a vet when he realised that the exams meant maths. But an aunt died, leaving him a little money—she was a member of an obscure religious sect; he assured me that she had returned to earth and still lived with him in the form of a stuffed Airedale—and he had decided to spend the rest of his life in tending animals in an amateur way. For that purpose he went for little walks, always carrying with him a thermometer and a used lolly-stick so that when he encountered an animal he could make it say 'Aaah!' and take its temperature. It was work he loved.

But, he confessed with a sudden flush, he had not as yet managed to examine an animal. No sooner had he pressed his used lolly-stick on the little, or large, or forked tongue than the creature sank its teeth into the nearest available piece of Oliver and was away. Not one 'Aaah!' had he achieved.

And worse than that, a blow from a robin's wing had lost him his arm. Oliver was up a ladder at the time, trying to take the temperature of this robin who was on a branch of an apple-tree. Apparently Oliver thought the robin looked rather flushed so approached it with his lolly-stick and said, 'Say "Aaah!" ' whereupon the robin flapped a wing which dislodged an apple which fell upon Oliver's fingers and he let go of the ladder.

Less obvious but just as regrettable was the loss of his left big toe when a tortoise he was trying to examine fell from his hands, and the loss of two medium toes on his right foot due to circumstances which I did not quite grasp but which entailed a rabbit and Oliver wearing green socks.

That was the last time I saw what was left of Oliver alive. I read an account of his passing over in a local paper I was folding up the other day (I had a hole in my shoe and it was coming on to rain). The newspaper report said that Oliver Sinclair Yarrop had bent down with a lolly-stick to a young lamb and was trying to persuade it to say 'Aaah!'. What Oliver had not noticed was that there was a large goat just behind him. But the goat had noticed Oliver. And the temptation was too great. It had charged.

As the coroner said, it was not the butt which hurt Oliver so much as the landing, which took an appreciable time to occur during which time Oliver was accelerating at the rate of thirty-two feet per sec. per sec. But what did the deceased think he was doing, fooling about with a lamb on the edge of Beachy Head?

So the forgettable Oliver died, and is almost forgotten. But if there is a hereafter, and I think there is, he will be happy at last. There will be green fields there. And hundreds and hundreds of little woolly lambs.

And more than that:

The lambs are going 'Aaah!' to Oliver Yarrop.

FROM *You Can't Have Your Kayak and Heat It*

The Story of Wong Ts'in and the Willow Plate Embellishment

by Ernest Bramah

Wong Ts'in, the rich porcelain-maker, was ill at ease within himself. He had partaken of his customary midday meal, flavoured the repast by unsealing a jar of matured wine, consumed a little fruit, a few sweetmeats and half a dozen cups of unapproachable tea, and then retired to an inner chamber to contemplate philosophically from the reposeful attitude of a reclining couch.

But upon this occasion the merchant did not contemplate restfully. He paced the floor in deep dejection and when he did use the couch at all it was to roll upon it in a sudden access of internal pain. The cause of his distress was well known to the unhappy person thus concerned, nor did it lessen the pangs of his emotion that it arose entirely from his own ill-considered action.

When Wong Ts'in had discovered, by the side of a remote and obscure river, the inexhaustible bed of porcelain clay that ensured his prosperity, his first care was to erect adequate sheds and labouring-places: his next to build a house sufficient for himself and those in attendance round about him.

So far prudence had ruled his actions, for there is a

keen edge to the saying: 'He who sleeps over his work-shop brings four eyes into the business,' but in one detail Wong Ts'in's head and feet went on different journeys, for with incredible oversight he omitted to secure the experience of competent astrologers and omen-casters in fixing the exact site of his mansion.

The result was what might have been expected. In excavating for the foundations, Wong Ts'in's slaves disturbed the repose of a small but rapacious earth-demon that had already been sleeping there for nine hundred and ninety-nine years. With the insatiable cunning of its kind, this vindictive creature waited until the house was completed and then proceeded to transfer its unseen but formidable presence to the quarters that were designed for Wong Ts'in himself. Thenceforth, from time to time, it continued to revenge itself for the trouble to which it had been put by an insidious persecution. This frequently took the form of fastening its claws upon the merchant's digestive organs, especially after he had partaken of an unusually rich repast (for in some way the display of certain viands excited its unreasoning animosity), pressing heavily upon his chest, invading his repose with dragon-dreams while he slept, and the like. Only by the exercise of an ingenuity greater than its own could Wong Ts'in succeed in baffling its ill-conditioned spite.

On this occasion, recognising from the nature of his pangs what was taking place, Wong Ts'in resorted to a stratagem that rarely failed him. Announcing in a loud voice that it was his intention to refresh the surface of his body by the purifying action of heated vapour, and then to proceed to his mixing-floor, the merchant withdrew. The demon, being an earth dweller with the ineradicable objection of this class of creatures towards all the elements of moisture, at once relinquished its hold, and going direct to the part of the works indicated, it there awaited its victim with the design of resuming its discreditable persecution.

Wong Ts'in had spoken with double tongue. On leaving the inner chamber he quickly traversed certain obscure passages of his house until he reached an inferior portal. Even if the demon had suspected his purpose it would not have occurred to a creature of its narrow outlook that anyone of Wong Ts'in's importance would make use of so menial an outway. The merchant therefore reached his garden unperceived and thenceforward maintained an undeviating face in the direction of the Outer Expanses. Before he had covered many li he was assured that he had indeed succeeded for the time in shaking off his unscrupulous tormentor. His internal organs again resumed their habitual calm and his mind was lightened as from an over-hanging cloud.

There was another reason why Wong Ts'in sought the solitude of the thinly-peopled outer places, away from the influence and distraction of his own estate. For some time past a problem that had once been remote was assuming dimensions of increasing urgency. This detail concerns Fa Fai, who had already been referred to by a person of literary distinction, in a poetical analogy occupying three written volumes, as a pearl-tinted peach-blossom shielded and restrained by the silken net-work of wise parental affection (and recognising the justice of the comparison, Wong Ts'in had been induced to purchase the work in question). Now that Fa Fai had attained an age when she could fittingly be sought in marriage, the contingency might occur at any time, and the problem confronting her father's decision was this: owing to her incomparable perfection Fa Fai must be accounted one of Wong Ts'in's chief possessions, the other undoubtedly being his secret process of simulating the lustrous effect of pure gold embellishment on china by the application of a much less expensive substitute. Would it be more prudent to concentrate the power of both influences and let it become known that with Fa Fai would go the essential part of his very remunerative clay enterprise, or would it be more prudent to divide these attractions and secure two distinct influences, both concerned about his welfare? In the first case there need be no reasonable limit to the extending vista of his ambition, and he might even aspire to greet as a son the highest functionary of the province—an official of such heavily-sustained importance that when he went about it required six chosen slaves to carry him, and of late it had been considered more prudent to employ eight.

If, on the other hand, Fa Fai went without any added inducement, a mandarin of moderate rank would probably be as high as Wong Ts'in could look, but he would certainly be able to adopt another of at least equal position, at the price of making over to him the ultimate benefit of his discovery. He could thus acquire either two sons of reasonable influence, or one who exercised almost unlimited authority. In view of his own childlessness, and of his final dependence on the services of others, which arrangement promised the most regular and liberal transmission of supplies to his expectant spirit when he had passed into the Upper Air, and would his connection with one very important official or with two subordinate ones secure him the greater amount of honour and serviceable recognition among the more useful deities?

To Wong Ts'in's logical mind it seemed as though there must be a definite answer to this problem. If one manner of behaving was right the other must be wrong, for as the wise philosopher Ning-hy was wont to say:

'Where the road divides there stand two Ning-hys.' The decision on a matter so essential to his future comfort ought not to be left to chance. Thus it had become a habit of Wong Ts'in's to penetrate the Outer Spaces in the hope of there encountering a specific omen.

Alas, it had been well written: 'He who thinks that he is raising a mound may only in reality be digging a pit.' In his continual search for a celestial portent among the solitudes Wong Ts'in had of late necessarily somewhat neglected his earthly (as it may be expressed) interests. In these emergencies certain of the more turbulent among his workers had banded themselves together into a confederacy under the leadership of a craftsman named Fang. It was the custom of these men, who wore a badge and recognised a mutual oath and imprecation, to present themselves before Wong Ts'in and demand a greater reward for their exertions than they had previously agreed to, threatening that unless this was accorded they would cast down the implements of their labour in unison and involve in idleness those who otherwise would have continued at their task. This menace Wong Ts'in bought off from time to time by agreeing to their exactions, but it began presently to appear that this way of appeasing them resembled Chou Hong's method of extinguishing a fire by directing jets of wind against it. On the day with which this story has so far concerned itself, a band of the most highly remunerated and privileged of the craftsmen had appeared before Wong Ts'in with the intolerable Fang at their head. These men were they whose skill enabled them laboriously to copy upon the surfaces of porcelain a given scene without appreciable deviation from one to the other, for in those remote cycles of history no other method was yet known or even dreamed of.

'Suitable greetings, employer of our worthless services,' remarked their leader, seating himself upon the floor unbidden. 'These who speak through the mouth of the cringing mendicant before you are the Bound-together Brotherhood of Colour-mixers and Putters-on of Thought-out Designs, bent upon a just cause.'

'May their Ancestral Tablets never fall into disrepair,' replied Wong Ts'in courteously. 'For the rest—let the mouth referred to shape itself into the likeness of a narrow funnel, for the lengthening gong-strokes press round about my unfinished labours.'

'That which in justice requires the amplitude of a full-sized cask shall be pressed down into the confines of an inadequate vessel,' assented Fang. 'Know then, O battener upon our ill-requited skill, how it has come to our knowledge that one who is not of our Brotherhood moves among us and performs an equal task for a less reward. This is our spoken word in consequence: in place of one tael every man among us shall now take two, and he who before has laboured eight gongs to receive it shall henceforth labour four. Furthermore, he who is speaking shall, as their recognised head and authority, always be addressed by the honourable title of "Polished", and the dog who is not one of us shall be cast forth.'

'My hand itches to reward you in accordance with the inner prompting of a full heart,' replied the merchant, after a well-sustained pause. 'But in this matter my very deficient ears must be leading my threadbare mind astray. The moon has not been eaten up since the day when you stood before me in a like attitude and bargained that every man should henceforth receive a full tael where hitherto a half had been his portion, and that in place of the toil of sixteen gong-strokes eight should suffice. Upon this being granted all bound themselves by spoken word that the matter should stand thus and thus between us until the gathering in of the next rice harvest.'

'That may have been so at the time,' admitted Fang, with dog-like obstinacy, 'but it was not then known that you had pledged yourself to Hien Nan for tenscore embellished plates of porcelain within a stated time, and that our services would therefore be essential to your reputation. There has thus arisen what may be regarded as a new vista of eventualities, and this frees us from the bondage of our spoken word. Having thus moderately stated our unbending demand, we will depart until the like gong-stroke of tomorrow, when, if our claim be not agreed to, all will cast down their implements of labour with the swiftness of a lightning-flash and thereby involve the whole of your too-profitable undertaking in well-merited stagnation. We go, venerable head; auspicious omens attend your movements!'

'May the All-Seeing guide your footsteps,' responded Wong Ts'in, and with courteous forbearance he waited until they were out of hearing before he added—'into a vat of boiling sulphur!'

Thus may the position be outlined when Wei Chang, the unassuming youth whom the black-hearted Fang had branded with so degrading a comparison, sat at his appointed place rather than join in the discreditable conspiracy, and strove by his unaided dexterity to enable Wong Ts'in to complete the tenscore embellished plates by the appointed time. Yet already he knew that in this commendable ambition his head grew larger than his hands, for he was the slowest-working among all Wong Ts'in's craftsmen, and even then his copy could frequently be detected from the original. Not to overwhelm his memory with unmerited contempt it is fitting now to reveal somewhat more of the unfolding curtain of events.

Wei Chang was not in reality a worker in the art of applying coloured designs to porcelain at all. He was a student of the literary excellences and had decided to devote his entire life to the engaging task of reducing the most perfectly matched analogy to the least possible number of words when the unexpected appearance of Fa Fai unsettled his ambitions. She was restraining the impatience of a powerful horse and controlling its movements by means of a leather thong, while at the same time she surveyed the landscape with a disinterested glance in which Wei Chang found himself becoming involved. Without stopping to consult the spirits of his revered ancestors on so important a decision, he at once burned the greater part of his collection of classical analogies and engaged himself, as one who is willing to become more proficient, about Wong Ts'in's earthyards. Here, without any reasonable intention of ever becoming in any way personally congenial to her, he was in a position occasionally to see the distant outline of Fa Fai's movements, and when a day passed and even this was withheld he was content that the shadow of the many-towered building that contained her should obscure the sunlight from the window before which he worked.

While Wei Chang was thus engaged the door of the enclosure in which he laboured was thrust cautiously inwards, and presently he became aware that the being whose individuality was never completely absent from his thoughts was standing in an expectant attitude at no great distance from him. As no other person was present, the craftsmen having departed in order to consult an oracle that dwelt beneath an appropriate sign, and Wong Ts'in being by this time among the Outer Ways seeking an omen as to Fa Fai's disposal, Wei Chang did not think it respectful to become aware of the maiden's presence until a persistent distress of her throat compelled him to recognise the incident.

'Unapproachable perfection,' he said, with becoming deference, 'is it permissible that in the absence of your enlightened sire you should descend from your golden eminence and stand, entirely unattended, at no great distance from so ordinary a person as myself?'

'Whether it may be strictly permissible or not, it is only on like occasions that she ever has the opportunity of descending from the solitary pinnacle referred to,' replied Fa Fai, not only with no outward appearance of alarm at being directly addressed by one of a different sex, but even moving nearer to Wei Chang as she spoke. 'A more essential detail in the circumstances concerns the length of time that he may be prudently relied upon to be away?'

'Doubtless several gong-strokes will intervene before his returning footsteps gladden our expectant vision,' replied Wei Chang. 'He is spoken of as having set his face towards the Outer Ways, there perchance to come within the influence of a portent.'

'Its probable object is not altogether unknown to the one who stands before you,' admitted Fa Fai, 'and as a dutiful and affectionate daughter it has become a consideration with her whether she ought not to press forward, as it were, to a solution on her own account . . . If the one whom I am addressing could divert his attention from the embellishment of the very inadequate claw of a wholly superfluous winged dragon, possibly he might add his sage counsel on that point.'

'It is said that a bull-frog once rent his throat in a well-meant endeavour to advise an eagle in the art of flying,' replied Wei Chang, concealing the bitterness of his heart

beneath an easy tongue. 'For this reason it is inexpedient
for earthlings to fix their eyes on those who dwell in very
high places.'

'To the intrepid, very high places exist solely to be
scaled; with others, however, the only scaling they attempt is lavished on the armour of preposterous flying
monsters, O youth of the House of Wei!'

'Is it possible,' exclaimed Wei Chang, moving forward
with so sudden an ardour that the maiden hastily withdrew herself several paces from beyond his enthusiasm,
'is it possible that this person's hitherto obscure and exe-
crated name is indeed known to your incomparable
lips?'

'As the one who periodically casts up the computations
of the sums of money due to those who labour about the
earth-yards, it would be strange if the name had so far
escaped my notice,' replied Fa Fai, with a distance in her
voice that the few paces between them very inadequately
represented. 'Certain details engrave themselves upon
the tablets of recollection by their persistence. For instance, the name of Fang is generally at the head of each
list; that of Wei Chang is invariably at the foot.'

'It is undeniable,' admitted Wei Chang, in a tone of
well-merited humiliation; 'and the attainment of never
having yet applied a design in such a manner that the
copy might be mistaken for the original has entirely
flattened out this person's self-esteem.'

'Doubtless,' suggested Fa Fai, with delicate encouragement, 'there are other pursuits in which you would disclose a more highly developed proficiency—as that of
watching the gyrations of untamed horses, for example.
Our more immediate need, however, is to discover a
means of defeating the malignity of the detestable Fang.
With this object I have for some time past secretly

applied myself to the task of contriving a design which, by blending simplicity with picturesque effect, will enable one person in a given length of time to achieve the amount of work hitherto done by two.'

With these auspicious words the accomplished maiden disclosed a plate of translucent porcelain, embellished in the manner which she had described. At the sight of the ingenious way in which trees and persons, stream and buildings, and objects of a widely differing nature had been so arranged as to give the impression that they all existed at the same time, and were equally visible without undue exertion on the part of the spectator who regarded them, Wei Chang could not restrain an exclamation of delight.

'How cunningly imagined is the device by which objects so varied in size as an orange and an island can be depicted within the narrow compass of a porcelain plate without the larger one completely obliterating the smaller or the smaller becoming actually invisible by comparison with the other! Hitherto this unimaginative person had not considered the possibility of showing other than dragons, demons, spirits and the forces which from their celestial nature may be regarded as possessing no real thickness or substance and therefore being particularly suitable for treatment on a flat surface. But this engaging display might indeed be a scene having an actual existence at no great space away.'

'Such is assuredly the case,' admitted Fa Fai. 'Within certain limitations, imposed by this new art of depicting realities as they are, we may be regarded as standing before an open window. The important-looking building on the right is that erected by this person's venerated father. Its prosperity is indicated by the luxurious profusion of the fruit-tree overhanging it. Pressed somewhat to the back, but of dignified proportion, are the outer buildings of those who labour among the clay.'

'In a state of actuality, they are of measurably less dignified dimensions,' suggested Wei Chang.

'The objection is inept,' replied Fa Fai. 'The buildings in question undoubtedly exist at the indicated position. If, therefore, the actuality is to be maintained, it is necessary either to raise their stature or to cut down the trees obscuring them. To this gentle-minded person the former alternative seemed the less drastic. As, however, it is regarded in a spirit of no-satisfaction—'

'Proceed, incomparable one, proceed,' implored Wei Chang. 'It was but a breath of thought, arising from a recollection of the many times that this incapable person has struck his unworthy head against the roof-beams of those nobly-proportioned buildings.'

'The three stunted individuals crossing the bridge in undignified attitudes are the debased Fang and two of his mercenary accomplices. They are, as usual, bending their footsteps in the direction of the hospitality of a house that announces its purpose beneath the sign of a spreading bush. They are positioned as crossing the river to a set purpose, and the bridge is devoid of a rail in the hope that on their return they may all fall into the torrent in a helpless condition and be drowned, to the satisfaction of the beholders.'

'It would be a fitting conclusion to their ill-spent lives,' agreed Wei Chang. 'Would it not add to their indignity to depict them as struggling beneath the waves?'

'It might do so,' admitted Fa Fai graciously, 'but in order to express the arisement adequately it would be necessary to display them twice—first on the bridge with their faces turned towards the west, and then in the flood with their faces towards the east; and the superficial might hastily assume that the three on the bridge would rescue the three in the river.'

'You are all-wise,' said Wei Chang, with well-marked admiration in his voice. 'This person's suggestion was opaque.'

'In any case,' continued Fa Fai, with a reassuring glance, 'it is a detail that is not essential to the frustration of Fang's malignant scheme, for already well on its way towards Hien Nan may be seen a trustworthy junk, laden with two formidable crates, each one containing fivescore plates of the justly esteemed Wong Ts'in porcelain.'

'Nevertheless,' maintained Wei Chang mildly, 'the out-passing of Fang would have been a satisfactory detail of the occurrence.'

'Do not despair,' replied Fa Fai. 'Not idly is it written: "Destiny has four feet, eight hands and sixteen eyes: how then shall the ill-doer with only two of each hope to escape?" An even more ignominious end may await Fang, should he escape drowning, for, conveniently placed by the side of the stream, this person has introduced a spreading willow-tree. Any of its lower branches is capable of sustaining Fang's weight, should a reliable rope connect the two.'

'There is something about that which this person now learns is a willow that distinguishes it above all the other trees of the design,' remarked Wei Chang admiringly. 'It has a wild and yet a romantic aspect.'

'This person had not yet chanced upon a suitable title for the device,' said Fa Fai, 'and a distinguished name is necessary, for possibly scores of copies may be made before its utility is exhausted. Your discriminating praise shall be accepted as a fortunate omen, and henceforth this shall be known as the Willow Pattern Embellishment.'

'The honour of suggesting the title is more than this commonplace person can reasonably carry,' protested Wei Chang, feeling that very little worth considering existed outside the earth-shed. 'Not only scores, but even hundreds of copies may be required in the process of time, for a crust of rice-bread and a handful of dried figs eaten from such a plate would be more satisfying than a repast of many-coursed richness elsewhere.'

In this well-sustained and painless manner Fa Fai and Wei Chang continued to express themselves agreeably to each other, until the lengthening gong-strokes warned the former person that her absence might inconvenience Wong Ts'in's sense of tranquillity on his return, nor did Wei Chang contest the desirability of a great space intervening between them should the merchant chance to pass that way. In the meanwhile Chang had explained many of the inner details of his craft so that Fa Fai should the better understand the requirements of her new art.

'Yet where is the Willow plate itself?' said the maiden, as she began to arrange her mind towards departure. 'As the colours were still in a receptive state this person placed it safely aside for a time. It was somewhat near the spot where you—'

During the amiable exchange of shafts of polished conversation Wei Chang had followed Fa Fai's indication and had seated himself upon a low bench without any very definite perception of his movements. He now arose with the unstudied haste of one who has inconvenienced a scorpion.

'Alas!' he exclaimed, in a tone of the acutest mental distress; 'can it be possible that this utterly profane outcast has so desecrated—'

'Certainly comment of an admittedly crushing nature

has been imposed upon this one's well-meant handiwork,' said Fa Fai. With these lightly-barbed words, which were plainly devised to restore the other person's face towards himself, the magnanimous maiden examined the plate which Wei Chang's uprising had revealed.

'Not only has the embellishment suffered no real detriment,' she continued, after an adequate glance, 'but there has been imparted to the higher lights—doubtless owing to the nature of the fabric in which your lower half is encased—a certain nebulous quality that adds greatly to the successful effect of the various tones.'

At the first perception of the indignity to which he had subjected the entrancing Fa Fai's work, and the swift feeling that much more than the coloured adornment of a plate would thereby be destroyed, all power of retention had forsaken Wei Chang's incapable knees and he sank down heavily upon another bench. From this dejection the maiden's well-chosen encouragement recalled him to a position of ordinary uprightness.

'A tombstone is lifted from this person's mind by your gracefully-placed words,' he declared, and he was continuing to indicate the nature of his self-reproach by means of a suitable analogy when the expression of Fa Fai's eyes turned him to a point behind himself. There, lying on the spot from which he had just risen, was a second Willow plate, differing in no detail of resemblance from the first.

'Shadow of the Great Image!' exclaimed Chang, in an awe-filled voice. 'It is no marvel that miracles should attend your footsteps, celestial one, but it is incredible that this clay-souled person should be involved in the display.'

'Yet,' declared Fa Fai, not hesitating to allude to things as they existed, in the highly-raised stress of the discovery, 'it would appear that the miracle is not specifically connected with this person's feet. Would you not, in furtherance of this line of suggestion, place yourself in a similar attitude on yet another plate, Wei Chang?'

Not without many protests that it was scarcely becoming thus to sit repeatedly in her presence, Chang complied with the request, and upon Fa Fai's further insistence he continued to impress himself, as it were, upon a succession of porcelain plates, with a like result. Not until the eleventh process was reached did the Willow design begin to lose its potency.

'Ten perfect copies produced within as many moments, and not one distinguishable from the first!' exclaimed Wei Chang, regarding the array of plates with pleasurable emotion. 'Here is a means of baffling Fang's crafty confederacy that will fill Wong Ts'in's ears with waves of gladness on his return.'

'Doubtless,' agreed Fa Fai, with a dark intent. She was standing by the door of the enclosure in the process of making her departure, and she regarded Wei Chang with a set deliberation. 'Yet,' she continued definitely, 'if this person possessed that which was essential to Wong Ts'in's prosperity, and Wong Ts'in held that which was necessary for this one's tranquillity, a locked bolt would be upon the one until the other was pledged in return.'

With these opportune words the maiden vanished, leaving Wei Chang prostrating himself in spirit before the many-sidedness of her wisdom.

Wong Ts'in was not altogether benevolently inclined towards the universe on his return a little later. The persistent image of Fang's overthreatening act still corroded the merchant's throat with bitterness, for on his right he saw the extinction of his business as unremunerative if he agreed, and on the left he saw the extinction of his business as undependable if he refused to agree.

Furthermore, the omens were ill-arranged.

On his way outwards he had encountered an aged man who possessed two fruit-trees, on which he relied for sustenance. As Wong Ts'in drew near, this venerable person carried from his dwelling two beaten cakes of dog-dung and began to bury them about the root of the larger tree. This action, on the part of one who might easily be a disguised wizard, aroused Wong Ts'in's interest.

'Why,' he demanded, 'having two cakes of dung and two fruit-trees, do you not allot one to each tree, so that they both may benefit and return to you their produce in the time of your necessity?'

'The season promises to be one of rigour and great need,' replied the other. 'A single cake of dung might not provide sufficient nourishment for either tree, so that both should wither away. By reducing life to a bare necessity I could pass from one harvest to another on the fruit of this tree alone, but if both should fail I am undone. To this end I safeguard my existence by ensuring that at least the better of the two shall thrive.'

'Peace attend your efforts!' said Wong Ts'in, and he began to retrace his footsteps, well content.

Yet he had not covered half the distance back when his progress was impeded by an elderly hag who fed two goats, whose milk alone preserved her from starvation. One small measure of dry grass was all that she was able to provide them with, but she divided it equally between them, to the discontent of both.

'The season promises to be one of rigour and great need,' remarked Wong Ts'in affably, for the being before him might well be a creature of another part who had assumed that form for his guidance. 'Why do you not therefore ensure sustenance to the better of the two goats by devoting to it the whole of the measure of dry grass? In this way you would receive at least some nourishment in return and thereby safeguard your own existence until the rice is grown again.'

'In the matter of the two goats,' replied the aged hag, 'there is no better, both being equally stubborn and perverse, though one may be finer-looking, and more vainglorious than the other. Yet should I foster this one to the detriment of her fellow, what would be this person's plight if haply the weaker died and the stronger broke away and fled! By treating both alike I retain a double thread on life, even if neither is capable of much.'

'May the Unseen weigh your labours!' exclaimed Wong Ts'in in a two-edged voice, and he departed.

When he reached his house he would have closed himself in his own chamber with himself had not Wei Chang persisted that he sought his master's inner ear with a heavy project. This interruption did not please Wong Ts'in, for he had begun to recognise the day as being unlucky, yet Chang succeeded by a device in reaching his side, bearing in his hands a guarded burden.

Though no written record of this memorable interview exists, it is now generally admitted that Wei Chang either involved himself in an unbearably attenuated caution before he would reveal his errand, or else that he made a definite allusion to Fa Fai with a too sudden conciseness, for the slaves who stood without heard Wong Ts'in clear his voice of all restraint and express himself freely on a variety of subjects. But this gave place to a subdued murmur, ending with the ceremonial breaking of a plate, and later Wong Ts-in beat upon a silver bell and called for wine and fruit.

The next day Fang presented himself a few gong-strokes later than the appointed time, and being met by an unbending word he withdrew the labour of those whom he controlled. Thenceforth these men, providing themselves with knives and axes, surrounded the gate of the earth-yards and by the pacific argument of their attitudes succeeded in persuading others who would willingly have continued at their task that the air of Wong Ts'in's sheds was not congenial to their health. Towards Wei Chang, whose efforts they despised, they raised a cloud of derision, and presently noticing that henceforth he invariably clad himself in lower garments of a dark blue material (to a set purpose that will be as crystal to the sagacious), they greeted his appearance with cries of: 'Behold the sombre one! Thou dark leg!' so that this reproach continues to be hurled even to this day at those in a like case, though few could answer why.

Long before the stipulated time the tenscore plates were delivered to Hien Nan. So greatly were they esteemed, both on account of their accuracy of unvarying detail and the ingenuity of their novel embellishment, that orders for scores, hundreds and even thousands began to arrive from all quarters of the Empire. The clay enterprise of Wong Ts'in took upon itself an added lustre, and in order to deal adequately with so vast an undertaking the grateful merchant adopted Wei Chang and placed him upon an equal footing with himself. On the same day Wong Ts'in honourably fulfilled his spoken word and the marriage of Wei Chang and Fa Fai took place, accompanied by the most lavish display of fireworks and coloured lights that the province had ever seen. The controlling deities approved, and they had seven sons, one of whom had seven fingers upon each hand. All these sons became expert in Wei Chang's process of transferring porcelain embellishment, for some centuries elapsed before it was discovered that it was not absolutely necessary to sit upon each plate to produce the desired effect.

This chronicle of an event that is now regarded as almost classical would not be complete without an added reference to the ultimate end of the sordid Fang.

Fallen into disrepute among his fellows owing to the evil plight towards which he had enticed them, it became his increasing purpose to frequent the house beyond the river. On his return at nightfall he invariably drew aside on reaching the bridge, well knowing that he could not prudently rely upon his feet among so insecure a crossing, and composed himself to sleep amidst the rushes. While in this position one night he was discovered and pushed into the river by a devout ox (an instrument of the high destinies), where he perished incapably.

Those who found his body, not being able to withdraw so formidable a weight direct, cast a rope across the lower branch of a convenient willow-tree and thus raised it to the shore. In this striking manner Fa Fai's definite opinion achieved a destined end.

FROM *Kai Lung's Golden Hours*

A Strategy Suit
with a Jelly Pocket

by Ivor Cutler

'I should like a strategy suit with a jelly pocket, please.'

'Strategy suits we have, sir, without jelly pockets. Ordinary suits *with* jelly pockets. Strategy suits *with* jelly pockets we don't have.'

'Well, I must say you seem indifferent to the needs of the public.'

'Nobody's ever asked me for a strategy suit with a jelly pocket before. A man who wants a strategy suit is a different man from him who wants a jelly pocket. Why not try next door?'

'I'll do that, and thank you. It's not often a tradesman recommends a rival—good afternoon!'

'Good afternoon.'

'I'd like a strategy suit with a jelly pocket, please.'

'How dare you, how dare you come into a place like this—an establishment like this, for a strategy suit with a jelly pocket. I've been a tailor for three generations. You want a strategy suit with a jelly pocket? Go next door!'

'I've just been next door.'

'No no! *He* doesn't have them. Go one down! Don't come bothering me again unless you want a proper suit. By Jupiter!'

'Good afternoon, I'd like a strategy suit with a j . . .'

'I know what you want. You want a strategy suit with a jelly pocket, don't you? Try next door.'

'I've just been ne . . .'

'Not up there. *Down* the road. Next door.'

'All right. Why don't you . . .'

'Get out of my shop, quick!'

'Yes?'

'I should like a strategy suit with a jelly pocket.'

'I'm sorry sir. I've never heard of jelly pockets. We only do the normal kind of suits. Would you like to see one?'

'No no! It *must* have a jelly pocket.'

'Well. Try next door.'

'But I've just come from . . .'

'No, no, no, no. Try next door, one down the street.'

'Thank you very much.'

'There's no shop there!'

'Oh, sorry. Bang bang! Hammer hammer! There you are.'

'I know what you want. You want a strategy suit with a jelly pocket, don't you? They all come to me for strategy suits with jelly pockets!'

'How did you know?'

'None of the other fellows in the street stock them. Keep sending them down the road till they come to me.'

'And do you *have* strategy suits with jelly pockets?'

'Of *course* I have strategy suits with jelly pockets. I'm delighted to do business with you, sir. What size of jelly pocket do you want?'

'About so big.'

(*Big laugh.*) 'Ah hahahaha! You'll never get a London tailor to sell you a jelly pocket that size. Not in a strategy suit.'

'Look, mister, I've got a big family of kids! I need a big jelly pocket.'

'Ah, ha, ha. I'm sorry. You see, a strategy suit's not strong enough to take a jelly pocket that size; not where the jelly pocket's being fitted.'

'I see. Well, what's the maximum size?'

'Oh, about this size.'

'Well, if you could make me one.'

'I don't need to make you one. I have one here made to measure.'

'Can I try it on?'

'Of course, of course. Try it on. There. Perfect fit, isn't it?'

'Yes, it is indeed. Just as though it's been made for me.'

'It *has* been made for you.'

'What do you mean. I've only just come in here.'

'I'm a master tailor. Don't question me or I'll throw you out of my shop and you won't find a suit like this in London at a price like this.'

'How much is it?'

'Nothing.'

'*Nothing?* I can't take a suit like this for nothing. It wouldn't be moral.'

'Aw, all right then. Give me ten per cent of the jelly.'

FROM *Cock-a-doodle-don't*

BACKGROUND NOTES

Aiken, Joan, *British*
SAFE AND SOUNDPROOF, *page 107*
Joan Aiken comes from a literary family and writes in a variety of
styles and media. Her first books were collections of short stories for
children. Then came a series for older children set in a pseudo-
historical England as it would have been had the Jacobites won the
'45 Rebellion, one of which, *The Whispering Mountain* (1968), won the
Guardian Award for children's literature. Her adult thrillers are
gaining increasing popularity and are now available in paperback,
including *The Butterfly Picnic*. The most recent is *Voices in an Empty
House* (1975). The story in this anthology has not previously appeared
in book form.

Berton, Pierre, *Canadian*
THE GREAT DETERGENT PREMIUM RACE, *page 9*
One of Canada's most versatile and controversial writers, Pierre
Berton was born in White Horse, Yukon. Three of his books,
Klondike, The Mysterious North and *The Last Spike*, won Governor
General's Awards for Creative Non-Fiction. *The Comfortable Pew*
(1966), a personal comment on the complacency of the Anglican
Church in Canada, was a Canadian bestseller. He has written for
radio, television, films and revue, for many years had a regular
column in the *Toronto Daily Star*, and holds a Stephen Leacock
Medal for Humour.

Bowman, W. E., *British*
TO THE RANKLING LA, *page 13*
The Ascent of Rum Doodle was published in 1956 when the first ascent
of Everest was still fresh in people's minds, and, to anyone who has
read it, reading the more serious mountaineering books of the old
school can never be quite the same again. A second book, *The Cruise
of the Talking Fish* (1957) did the same for ocean voyages such as *The
Kon Tiki Expedition*. Both are now out of print.

Bramah, Ernest (1868–1942), *British*
THE STORY OF WONG TS'IN AND THE
WILLOW PLATE EMBELLISHMENT, *page 149*
Ernest Bramah (real name Ernest Bramah Smith), was a retiring
figure who shunned publicity, but as far as is known had never visited

China. His books about Kai Lung, an itinerant story-teller of Imperial China, were published over forty years: *The Wallet of Kai Lung* (1900), *Kai Lung's Golden Hours* (1922) in which this story is found within the story called 'The Inexorable Justice of the Mandarin Shan Tien', *Kai Lung Unrolls His Mat* (1928) and *Kai Lung beneath the Mulberry Tree* (1940). Bramah's style of using an exaggeration of the Chinese convention of elaborate, courteous but often double-tongued under-statement has long had an appeal to a minority who appreciate the peculiar, sophisticated humour.

Campbell, Patrick, *Irish*
TOOKING FOR A LOWEL, *page 76*
Patrick Campbell, the third Baron Glenavy, was born in 1913. He has had a regular column in the *Sunday Times* since 1961 and has also appeared on television panel shows and written for this medium and films. This piece first appeared in *Lilliput*, where he was assistant editor, before being collected in *Patrick Campbell's Omnibus* (1954, o.p.). His other books include *The P-P-Penguin Patrick Campbell* (1965, o.p.) and *My Life and Easy Times* (1967).

Crump, Barry, *New Zealand*
CAR EPISODE, *page 31*
This story is the opening chapter of *Hang on a Minute, Mate* (1963, o.p.), the picaresque adventures of Jack Lilburn and Sam Cash in rural New Zealand. Barry Crump has written a number of other books, but this remains the best known.

Cutler, Ivor, *British*
A STRATEGY SUIT WITH A JELLY POCKET, *page 169*
Ivor Cutler claims he is the only oblique musical philosopher (O.M.P.) there is. He won a competition for it in a place called Y'Hup, to get to which you 'sail up the W. side of S. America keeping 700–800 miles off the seashore till you come to it. It is green.' He has appeared in films, revue and cabaret, produced two books of work first broadcast on the B.B.C., three records of his musings and *Meal One*, a zany short story for children, illustrated by Helen Oxenbury (1971).

Gilbreth, Frank B. and Carey, Ernestine Gilbreth, *American*
MOTION STUDY TONSILS, *page 60*
This story is taken from *Cheaper by the Dozen* (1949) in which two of the Gilbreth children describe how their father applied his job efficiency techniques to his family's upbringing. The dedication is 'To DAD who only reared twelve children *and* to MOTHER who reared twelve only children.' Its popularity led to a sequel *Belles on their Toes* (1954), now out of print.

Henry, O. (1862–1910), *American*
THE GIFT OF THE MAGI, *page 81*
Real name William Sidney Porter, he was born in North Carolina, went to Texas as a young man and started writing while in prison for embezzling bank funds (a crime now thought to be due as much to his employers' negligence as his own). After his release he lived mainly in New York and wrote a story a week for magazines for many years, the simple plots about ordinary people with the twist of a surprise ending having a wide appeal. Collections of the stories are available in various editions.

Hollowood, Bernard, *British*
THE SPORTSMEN OF SCOWLE, *page 88*
Bernard Hollowood was born in Staffordshire in 1910, and like Stephen Leacock lectured in economics before turning to humour. Elected a member of the 'Table' of Punch in 1945 (where his articles and drawings appeared under the name of 'Hod'), he was the magazine's editor 1957–68. He played cricket for his home county and now writes a column in the Saturday edition of the *Daily Telegraph*. This excerpt is from *Scowle and Other Papers* (1948).

Jerome, Jerome K. (1859–1927), *British*
THE ADVANTAGES OF CHEESE AS A
TRAVELLING COMPANION, *page 122*
Three Men in a Boat, from which this is taken, was one of two books by the author published in 1889 and in the next decade he was a prolific writer and editor. A sequel, *Three Men on the Bummel* (1900), about a bicycle tour of Germany by the same characters, was never as popular, but Jerome later added to his reputation as a playwright, especially with *The Passing of the Third Floor Back* (1908), an up-dated morality play.

Leacock, Stephen (1869–1944), *Canadian*
'Q.' A PSYCHIC PSTORY OF THE PSUPERNATURAL, *page 48*
Born in England but taken to Canada as a child, Stephen Leacock was Dow Professor of Political Economy at McGill University, Montreal, 1908–36, and his *Elements of Political Science* (1906) became a classic text in this field. His first humorous book, *Literary Lapses*, was published privately in 1910, but soon taken by John Lane, the Bodley Head. Other titles included *Nonsense Novels* (1911) and *Frenzied Fiction* (1917).

Milne, A. A. (1882–1956), *British*
THE ARRIVAL OF BLACKMAN'S WARBLER, *page 37*
A. A. Milne is now best known for his stories and poems for children about Christopher Robin and Winnie the Pooh, and for his adaptation of part of Kenneth Grahame's *Wind in the Willows* into the play

Toad of Toad Hall. Long before that he had been a regular contributor to *Punch* and many of his humorous pieces had appeared in book form, of which *If I May* and *Those Were the Days* are still available. He also wrote a detective story *The Red House Mystery* (new edition 1971) and his autobiography, *It's Too Late Now.*

Muir, Frank, *British*
'THE LAMPS ARE GOING OUT ALL OVER EUROPE',
page 145
With Denis Norden, Frank Muir wrote the scripts of *Take It from Here*, a radio revue series in the fifties and sixties. More recently they have become performers in their own right on radio and television either separately, or together in two panel games, *My Music*, and *My Word* which is broadcast in Britain and the B.B.C. World Service and networked in over thirty-five other countries of the world. A second collection of these stories, *Upon My Word*, was published in 1974.

Nash, Ogden (1902–1971), *American*
THE STRANGE CASE OF MR DONNYBROOK'S BOREDOM,
page 93
Ogden Nash's light verses, which usually rhyme but do not necessarily scan, have often appeared in periodicals, including *The New Yorker*, before being collected in book form. His books include *Collected Verses, 1929 on* (1961), *There's Always Another Windmill* (1969) and *Bed Riddance* (1971).

O'Connor, Frank (1903–1966), *Irish*
FIRST CONFESSION, *page 96*
Frank O'Connor (real name Michael O'Donovan) is regarded as one of the best short story writers of this century, who according to W. B. Yeats, 'was doing for Ireland what Chekhov did for Russia'. A perfectionist, he frequently re-wrote his stories before and after publication and many have a rich vein of humour. *The Stories of Frank O'Connor*, from which this version is taken, is published by Hamish Hamilton (1953). *Collections Two* and *Three* (1964, 1969, paper-backs under other titles) are the definitive editions.

Parker, Dorothy (1893–1967), *American*
THE STANDARD OF LIVING, *page 41*
Described by Alexander Woollcott as 'a combination of Little Nell and Lady Macbeth', Dorothy Parker had an acid wit and ready tongue which gained her a wide reputation as a formidable literary critic ('This is not a novel to be tossed aside lightly. It should be thrown with great force'). and as a member of the 'Round Table' at the Algonquin Hotel, New York, in the twenties and thirties. Her

verse and stories, usually light and mocking in style but with reflective undertones, are available in *The Collected Dorothy Parker* (1973).

Runyon, Damon (1880–1946), *American*
TOBIAS THE TERRIBLE, *page 132*
Born in Manhattan, Kansas, Runyon achieved success in Manhattan, New York, as a newspaper reporter, especially of sporting events where he met characters which he later used as the basis of his short stories. His tough gangsters, with their distinctive slang and weaknesses for the soft touch or the fair sex, made their originator famous. A musical *Guys and Dolls* (also the title of the first book of stories, 1931) was produced on Broadway in 1952 and later made into a film. The stories are now available in two omnibus volumes, *Runyon on Broadway* (1950) and *Runyon from First to Last* (1954).

Stivens, Dal, *Australian*
THE SCHOLARLY MOUSE, *page 127*
Short stories by Dal Stivens have appeared in many periodicals in *Coast to Coast* anthologies of Australian short stories, one volume of which he edited. *The Scholarly Mouse* also appears in *Australian Short Stories, Second Series* in the Oxford World Classics. The author lives in Lingfield, New South Wales.

Thurber, James (1894–1961), *American*
THE NIGHT THE BED FELL, *page 25*
My Life and Hard Times, from which this episode was taken, is now available in Volume Two of *Vintage Thurber* (1963). This volume also includes *Further Fables for our Time* and *Thurber Carnival*, with some characteristic Thurber dogs. Much of the work originally appeared in the *New Yorker*.